AQUINAS LOCKE PEWTER

These superbly wrought English pewter goblets are hand made in Sheffield to a traditional Georgian design. Their exquisite outlines have restfulness and simplicity that combine to grace any table-setting whether traditional or contemporary. Pewter with its unique lustre enhances the pleasures of fine wines, draws out the full flavour of ales and beers. "Once the plate of Kings" pewter remains today a possession still very much to be prized.

Georgian Goblets

LARGE:
Set of six Goblets:	£15. 4.6	post free
Pair of Goblets:	£ 5. 0.0	plus 4/6 P.P.
Single Goblet:	£ 2.13.6	plus 2/6 P.P.

MEDIUM:
Set of six Goblets:	£13.18.6	post free
Pair of Goblets:	£ 4.15.0	plus 4/6 P.P.
Single Goblet:	£ 2.18.6	plus 2/6 P.P.

SMALL:
Set of six Goblets:	£11.18.6	post free
Pair of Goblets:	£ 4. 2.6	plus 4/6 P.P.
Single Goblet:	£ 2. 2.6	plus 2/6 P P.

Please place orders early for Christmas.
Send cash with order or pay C.O.D.

	Capacity:	Height:	Weight:
LARGE	10 fluid oz	6½ inches	8½ oz
MEDIUM	7 fluid oz	5½ inches	5 oz
SMALL	3 fluid oz	4 inches	3½ oz

Aquinas Locke & Company
Leighton Buzzard, Beds, ENGLAND.
Tel Leighton Buzzard 2027

Every week is Peter Scott week.

PS last word in Scottish knitwear
Peter Scott & Co. Ltd. Buccleuch St. Hawick Scotland

EXMOOR National Park

Heddon's Mouth

Exmoor, though one of the smallest of the National Parks, is unequalled in its variety of scene and mood. So contrasting are its many faces that a lifetime of exploration cannot exhaust its capacity to surprise. This booklet, addressed to those who live in the Park as well as those who visit it, describes the scenery of the moors and coast, plant and animal life, agriculture, human settlement, literary associations, recreations and places of interest. It contains an Ordnance Survey 2½-inch map for the Park area, a geological map and 23 plates.

(National Park Guide No 8)

8s 6d (by post 9s 2d)

For free lists of titles on guide books please write to Her Majesty's Stationery Office, P6A (CM), Atlantic House, Holborn Viaduct, London ECIP IBN

HMSO

Government publications can be bought from the Government Bookshops in London (post orders to PO Box 569 SE1), Edinburgh, Cardiff, Belfast, Manchester, Birmingham, and Bristol or through booksellers

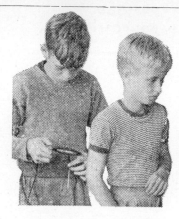

SPECIAL COUNTRYMAN SELECTION
IDEAL GIFT FOR THOSE INTERESTED
IN THE COUNTRYSIDE & NATURE

These quality volumes of fine photographs and text have been bound economically to give our readers an exceptional money-saving offer.

The autobiography of Peter Scott—naturalist, ornithologist, painter, naval officer, glider pilot, yachtsman, traveller, broadcaster and author—was first published in 1961. The author has added new material and particular emphasis is given to his more adventurous exploits and to his work for the Wildfowl Trust. Peter Scott's happy and diverse personality comes clearly through the pages of THE EYE OF THE WIND.

In this book Dr Richard Philps describes with vivid and infectious enthusiasm the way he sets about the job of coming within viewing distance of the shy and alert creatures that live in our woods, streams and hedgerows. The text is copiously illustrated with action photographs and diagrams.

(Richard Philps awarded Council of Nature prize for his films on methods of approaching and watching wild life.)

CONTENTS

REGULAR FEATURES

TEXT ILLUSTRATORS

ROBIN TANNER, Cover; PATRICIA FROST, 253; E. HERMLE, 266-269; R. GRIMSHAW, 272; SUE WHITAKER, 289-291; ROSEMARY WISE, 295; D. POCHIN MOULD, 298-301; ROSEMARY UPTON, 305; BRIAN WALKER, 323-325; ROBERT GILLMOR, 328-332; LEONARD AND MARJORIE GAYTON, 353; M. KAY-ROBINSON, 355-358; STANLEY BOND, 371.

EDITORIAL OFFICE, Burford Oxford, OX8 4LH (Oxford 19 miles; Cheltenham 22 miles). *Tel. Burford (099-382)* 2258. Closed Saturdays.

 SUBSCRIPTIONS AND BACK NUMBERS: Watling Street, Bletchley, Bucks. *Tel. Bletchley (09-082) 4921.* ADVERTISEMENTS: 23-27 Tudor Street, London E.C.4. *Tel. 01-583 9199*

PUBLISHED quarterly in March, June, September and December. The next issue will be out on March 3. THE COUNTRYMAN is obtainable from newsagents at 6s a copy. Annual subscription rates: Inland 30s, Overseas $5.00 or equivalent in your currency, post paid anywhere in the world.

TO CONTRIBUTORS. *Unaccepted contributions* returned only if accompanied by fully stamped and addressed envelope (overseas contributions international postage coupons). MSS stand a better chance if typewritten. *Drawings* should be on good board, preferably in Indian ink, and about twice the size to which they are likely to be reduced, with suggested caption and sender's name and address in full on the back. *Photographic prints* should be glossy bromide, with sharp detail, preferably unmounted, with name and address and description in soft pencil and should not be fastened with clips. Very small photographs should be accompanied by the negatives of the prints. *Photographs that have appeared or are on offer elsewhere not accepted.* No responsibility taken for drawings, photographs or literary contributions during transmission or in Editor's hands, and receipt of proof is no guarantee of appearance.

Are you a member of the National Trust?

We hope we are preaching to the converted, so as a good countryman (or woman) why not join the National Trust today?

The National Trust already protects half a million acres of our finest countryside and 300 miles of unspoilt coastline. They are safe for ever – but the threat to our environment becomes daily more menacing.

The Trust is a charity, a group of individuals acting for the nation, and it needs your support.

Ordinary membership of the Trust costs £2 a year and gives you the right of free entry to more than 200 properties the public pays to visit. There are reduced rates for juniors and families.

If you are already a member, why not give a year's subscription for a Christmas or a birthday present, or persuade your friends to join?

To: The National Trust, 23 Caxton Street, London s w 1

Please enrol me as a member of the National Trust:

I enclose £........................ for one year's subscription

MY NAME...

ADDRESS...

....

☐ Please send me details of junior and family membership

NT CODE: #

The Countryman

A Quarterly Non-Party Review
and Miscellany of Rural Life and Work
for the English-speaking World

*Founded by J. W. Robertson Scott and Edited
by John Cripps at Burford in Oxfordshire*

Volume 75   No 2   Winter 1970

Forty Years a Butler
by John Corkoran

*A manuscript, 'Memoirs of an Old English Family', with the
above subtitle, was found among papers of William Roscoe,
Liverpool city father (1753-1831), whose great-great-grand-
daughter, Mrs F. Lee-Michell, sent it to us.   A preamble,
which in style suggests that of an eighteenth-century pseudo-
autobiographical novel, states that the paper was given by
John Corkoran to his doctor on his death-bed 'and is copied
verbatim'.   The detailed description of 'Hartington Hall' does
not fit the Derbyshire seat of that name; but, whether fact or
fiction, the chapter provides a vivid picture of life in a country
house of the period.*

I AM seventy-two come St Swithuns, and am, God be
praised therefore, hale and stout and of sound
mind.   My eyes to be sure are not what they were
when I first cleaned the plate for the old Squires
wedding dinner, and could have seen the wing of a
midge in the chasings.

My father had been woodman to old Squire Hartington father of the old Squire and grandfather of the
young Squire that is.   He died of sitting all day in a

wet shirt when I was two years old, and my Mother she took to washing. The old Squire built her a laundry and sent her all the washing from the Hall, and I, for I was a handy lad, used to help her to wash. The lads at old Reading's school when I played marbles with them used to ask me to hold up my fingers which were white and rough with the soap and hot water and used to call me Suds, but I didn't mind them for my Mother was a kind Mother to me and I would have washed off my skin to have pleasured her.

May be the reader may think I learned to write at Reading's but if he does he's wrong for Reading could not write himself, and there wer'nt at that time more than four persons in the village that could, and they were the Curate, the Doctor, Mrs Williams the Chandler's wife and fat Tony Arrack who kept the Coach-horse and Fig-tree. Some said indeed that Davy Webster the parish Clerk could write, and so he used to say himself in the tap-room of the Coach-horse and Fig-tree, but nobody ever saw him make a pot-hook. No, no, it would have been thought a strange tale in the year 58 for such like as me to have been learning to write. No, no, I didn't learn till I was sixty, when Miss Elizabeth, God bless her kind heart and pretty face, it was the sweetest mildest thing I ever looked upon, took all the pains of teaching my old cramped fingers. "John" said she one afternoon when I was asking Mr Walter to write me some labels for the Sherry (Mr Walter minded the wine-cellar more than any of them, not that he was too fond of his glass, neither) "John" says she, "if you would like to learn to write yourself, I'll teach you." I thanked her kindly but told her I feared it was past my endeavour; but she bade me never fear but bid me come an hour before supper into the little Cedar parlour, and there night after night and week after week did my kind

young mistress teach me, till at last I wrote a plainer
hand than ever Tony Arrack did. But let me see,
where was I?

Well! it was a glorious spring morning, I think as I
write I smell the smell of the hawthorn-hedge upon
which I was spreading the cloathes which my Mother
and I had just wrung out, when I heard the yelping of
a little spaniel, and presently on the other side of the
hedge up rode the old Squire, and surely he was a
comely man of his years to see, though something too
apt to give those he didn't like a wipe with the rough
side of his tongue. He was very fat and pursy, and
joking thereabout he used to ask Jacob Gristley the
Miller whenever he met him if he dared weigh him in
the Mill scales without fresh ropes. Well! the Squire
rode up with his overlapping red cheeks as ruddy as an
August apple. "Hi! my lad" says he in his deep husky
voice (I think the old October he was so fond of had
affected his speaking a little), "how's thy Mother?" I
made a leg and thanked his Worship and called her.
"Good day, Molly Corkoran" said he "this is a likely
lad of yours, and we want just such another at the
Hall, send him there this morning and Jonathan shall
see whether he'll serve." My Mother curtsied and
thanked him, but I saw the tear was standing in her
eye for its a hard thing for a lone widow-woman to part
with an only child. As soon as the cloathes were all
spread, and I had eaten my bit of bacon, my Mother
bid me put on my Sunday coat and make haste to the
Hall.

It would take a better penman than an old Butler to
describe Hartington Hall, howsoever I'll do my best.
It lay about a mile from the highway, and the road to
it ran through a broad avenue of the finest and largest
Elms I ever saw. The gates of the Avenue were of
old-fashioned iron-work and swung on two massy

pillars of red brick at the top of each of which stood a
Leopard with an arrow in his paw which was the
Hartington arms like. The house itself was a true
ancient pile, all the gable-ends in the front, and
stacks of chimneys that looked like a town. Some said
it was built in the time of King Harry, but I heard
Dr Prial one day after dinner tell my Master, and
surely he had a right to know for there was not a
cranny in all the Garrets that he had not poked into
(he was what they call an Antiquarry) that he was sure
the Hall wasn't older than Bloody Queen Mary's time.
But Master didn't like that for he used always to tell
strangers that Sir Geoffrey Hartington had feasted
King Harry in the long gallery.

At the back of the house was the noblest Garden
in the county all walled in with a red brick wall
fourteen feet high covered with moss and fruit trees.
It was laid out to be sure in the most elegant and tasty
style of any garden I ever saw. All along the back of
the house there ran a broad gravel terrace guarded
with a stout stone balustrade, from which a flight of
steps led to the great grass walk. At the bottom of the
steps stood the Leopards with the arrows on both
sides. The great grass walk ran in a straight line to the
other end of the garden, marry, more than a quarter of
a mile where it ended in the pleasantest Alcove you
ever set your eyes upon. Twenty thousand pretty
creeping plants had fastened themselves amongst the
old stones and had grown all over the top of it so that
they hung down in sweet smelling garlands. In the
middle of the Alcove there stood an old rough table of
oak. Aye! many was the happy birthday feasts I have
seen spread upon that stout old board, when my
young Masters and Mistresses used to make holyday
work for one another. Lord! how happy I've seen
'em—eight ruddy lads and lasses all as merry as the

morning—and then to see 'em as I have seen them
since.   But Gods good will be done!

At the Alcove the great grass walk branched off
into two narrower ones.   From the end of the right-
hand walk you entered surely the sweetest shady place
that could be for a summers day.   First of all you came
into a round arbour which was quite covered with
Ladys-bower and Jessamine and it led you into a long
smooth walk covered in with old nut-trees, which only
let in just as much light as was sufficient to keep the
grass green.   At the other end was a little flower
garden the walks of which were made in the shape of
the figure H for Hartington and all flagged with white
flags, which looked pretty enough to be sure.   The
walk was called "the Hazels" or sometimes "the Lower
Hazles" and surely I may say it wasn't miscalled for
many a bit of courting has gone on there to my knowledge.   Indeed the day after I was put in livery Mrs
Merryweather the housekeeper sent me to gather some
filberts for the desert, and just as I got into the hazles
who should I see but the young squire that then was
and Miss Euphemy my mistress that after was, who
both jumped when they saw me as if I'd been a thief.
And by the same token many a pleasant five minutes
have I and pretty Bessy Gray that was Lady's Maid to
my old Mistress when she was young passed under the
shade of those nut-trees.   But Bessy was giddy and at
last ran away with Joe—I mean Joseph Crane my old
Masters groom.

Where was I? for my head is not as clear as it was
forty year ago.   Aye now I remember.   Well I set off
for the Hall as my mother bid me but I didn't half like
it.   I had sometimes been there with the linen for my
Mother but had never got beyond the scullery, much
less been *carpeted* as we used to say in the neighbourhood
when we had any of us been sent for into the rooms

where the family lived.   When I got to the Hall I was
told to go to the Squires own parlour which was a small
low room between the housekeepers room and the
Cedar Parlour with a couple of fowling-pieces over the
Chimney-piece.   When the footman opened the door
to let me in there was Joseph the Butler with the
Squire.   Mr Joseph was very like the Squire and
about his age only not quite so fat.   He had travelled
abroad in foreign parts with the Squire in his youth
and had lived with him ever since, and as the Squire
didn't keep much company he was always fond of
talking to Joseph about ancient times.   Mr Joseph
was standing up when I came in but there was a chair
close beside him, and there were two glasses on the
table and I think he had been sitting and helping the
Squire with the October. "Here Joseph" said the
Squire "here's Jack Corkoran. Can you lick him
into shape think you?"   "Please your Honour I'll try"
said Mr Joseph. "Well then" said the Squire "give him a
livery."   "I think, please your Honour" answered
Joseph "that Tom Bottom's will just fit him and its
only a month old."   I didn't like to hear this for I
knew that Tom Bottom had died of the Typhus—but
howsoever he hadn't given it to his Coat.

And so now I was fairly fixed in my service and I
tried to do my duty honestly and well.   I cleaned the
Squires and the young Squires shoes and Mr Josephs,
and Jonas the youngest footman made me clean his.
I cleaned the knives too and sometimes the plate, and
brushed the young squires cloathes and waited on him
when he was dressing and stood behind his chair at
dinner.   And altogether I lived very comfortably
though Jonas took a spite against me and did me an ill
turn whenever he could.   I remember one time
when my young Master was going to an archery
Meeting, at which Miss Euphemy was to give a silver

arrow to the best shot he told me I should go with him
to carry his arrows.   Now Jonas was jealous of this
and what does he do but gets Sam Gregory the postillion
who was driving the Squire to the Town to buy him
something at the Druggists, and on the Archery
morning as he was carrying the Coffee out of the
Parlour he says to me "Come Jack, thou'lt maybe get
nothing till night, I'll give thee a drop of Coffee" and
so he takes me into the Pantry and gives me a cup.
My mind misgave me as I drank it for it was preciously
bitter but he told me it was Turkey which always had
that taste and so I drank it up.   In about half an hour
I grew so sick and cold that I went and stood in the
Servants hall with my back against the wall which was
always hot for the kitchen fire was at the other side.
But this made me no better and when the young
Squire sent for me I couldn't go and so he took Jonas
with him in my place.   But all this didn't answer for
Jonas after all.   I was sick all morning and Mrs
Merryweather ordered Molly the Scullion to boil three
quarts of thin oat-meal gruel all of which she made me
drink—which if I hadn't been sick would have made
me so, but as it was it made me well.

   The young Squire was a good shot and he won the
Silver arrow, and everybody said it was the prettiest
sight in the world to see Miss Euphemy smile as she
gave it to him in the middle of all the handsomest
young Ladies and Gentlemen in the County.   And so
things went on till at last orders were given for everything to be got ready for the young Squires wedding.
And sure enough it was sharp work for the Servants
for though the Squire had none but very distant
relations yet he thought it right on so grand an occasion
to have the Hall as full as it could hold.   Miss Euphemy,
you see, she was the Squires ward, and had but few
friends; only her Uncle a proud poor old Gentleman

and rather hard-favoured came down from Scotland to give her away.

Well, as the wedding-day came nearer we had all to work the harder, and my Mother she was sent for to scour the spare bed-rooms. Mr Joseph perspired wonderfully in polishing the Great Dining tables which he said would be a disgrace to the Hall and him if he could not get ready by the wedding-day. Then there was a lot of old plate which had lain by since Mr Harry was christened, and that again took a power of polishing. Mr Joseph all along said it would kill him, and very down-hearted he was but he would have done twice as much for the honour of the old Hall and Mr Harry. I think if he hadn't drunk so much of the new brew while he was polishing the tables it would have been better for him for he was obliged to stoop his head, and then all the blood would rush into his face yet he would scrub till he staggered. We had all of us new liveries and Jonathan the Coachman had a new wig also. And indeed he deserved it, for he had taken wonderful pains to furbish up the old coach.

It was a glorious wedding. First went the old Master, and my young Ladys Uncle and my young Lady and one of the bride-maids in the family coach. And behind it were Thomas and Jonas. Then came the young Squire in his own carriage with two Oxford Scholars who were friends of him. And behind this I rode. And after this came Mr Hammond Hartingtons carriage, but he did not come to the Wedding himself, for the old Squire and he didn't agree about their pedigree Mr Hammond maintaining he was the older branch—and sure enough, much evil came of this. After Mr Hammonds came four more coaches with the best gentry in the neighbourhood.

Oh what a wedding dinner there was! Fifty four Ladies and Gentlemen sate down in the long Gallery

for the Dining room was too small for them—and all
the Tenants and their wives and daughters were feasted
with roast beef and plumb-pudding in the Servants
Hall.   When the bride and bridegrooms health was
drunk with three times three by the gentlefolk in the
gallery it was answered by such a cheer from the
Servants Hall (for there was not a soul on the Estate
that wasn't fond of Mr Harry) that you would have
thought all the old rafters of the Hall would have
given way.

The young Squire determined to take his Bride to
see all the wonders of London, and says he to me "John"
says he "you have behaved yourself well, and you shall
go with me to London as my valet"—and surely we had
a pleasant journey and wonderfully civil were all the
landlords on the road.   But when we got to London
we found it all in an uproar about one Mr Wilkes and
45 something or other but I never could learn what.
However my Master said that Mr Wilkes was the
guardian of our rights and so whenever I got into the
crowds I used to flourish my hat and shout Wilkes and
Liberty!   After we had been a little time in London
Master and Mistress went to Court and though I
was their servant I will say it, a handsomer pair were
never seen in the Kings Palace.   Sir Jacob Greenvill
dined with my Master the day after they had been at
Court, and I heard him tell Master that the young King
said when he saw my Mistress "Pretty woman, pretty
woman; who is she, who is she?"   And my Master was
mightily pleased.

When we had been in London about a fortnight
and I was beginning to be able to find my way, one
night about twelve o'clock just when my Master and
Mistress had got back from old Drury there comes a
loud knock at the door and when I opened it in walked
Sam Gregory all spattered with mud from crown to

heel with a letter for my Master. I asked him what was
to do but he bade me run with it to Master as hard as
I could and so I did.   He was sitting alone and as soon
as he opened it his cheeks grew as white as a pair of
bleached sheets.   I thought he was going to faint and
was running for some brandy, but he bade me stay
and pressing his forehead with both hands he told me
to read the note aloud to him for that he could not see
the Letters, and yet there was not a single tear in his
eyes.   And sure enough he might well take on so as I
soon found, for the news was grievous.   The letter
was from Joseph and was something as follows.

Honoured Mr Harry.

Oh my poor Master! He was getting a-horseback
yesterday when he was struck with a stroke. He has never
spoken since but two words and they were "Where's
Harry?" The Doctor says there's little hope.   God bless
you, dear Mr Harry do come to the Hall as fast as you can
while Master is alive.   If he dies I think I shall shortly
follow him.

                    Your Honours humble servant to command
                              Joseph Johnson.
My humble service to my young mistress.

As soon as Mr Harry could get his thoughts to rights
again he called a chaise, and in less than twenty
minutes my mistress and he in all their gay dresses
were on their melancholy way home.   It was a sad
shock for him for he had been an only child, and the
old Squire and he had lived as if there had been nobody
else in the world.   When he got to the Hall my poor
old Master had been cold ten hours, and Joseph too
he had sickened and taken to his bed.   The young
Squire in all his grief was very kind to him, but he said
he had no wish to live and he was buried just a week
after the old Squire in Hartington Churchyard.

Well! this made the Squire settle down at the Hall which he hadn't intended to do for a year or two yet for he talked of taking my Mistress over the seas to see foreign parts. But when the old Squire died he would not leave his servants without a master and his tenants without a Landlord and so he determined to stay at home. And now as Joseph was dead Jonas thought he ought to be made butler, but he was jealous of me and tried to set my master against me. But it wouldn't do, for one day he got so drunk before dinner that he upset all the soup over Mrs Pewsey the Rectors wife, and Master saw what was the matter with him and turned him off the next morning. I heard afterwards that he was hanged to Tyburn Turnpike for trying to poison a gentleman he was footman to in London, but whether it was so or not I can't justly say.

One morning when I was taking my master his boots says he "John, I have found you faithful and honest, and I shall make you my Butler." And so I was taken out of livery and was made Butler—a sort of honourable promotion that few so young as I was have met with.

Snow

IT snows in my soul as it snows on the ground;
    And the cold in my soul is the cold in the sound
Of a snow-laden wind from a maiden-white cloud.

Very fine are the flakes,
Very soft is the fall;
Mother-soft fingers are weaving a shawl,
Are folding a shawl where an orphaned heart aches.

Phoebe Hesketh

The Man Who Made Things Grow
by Donald M. McFarlan

NOT long before the disastrous Biafran war I sat in
the doctor's bungalow at Uburu in Eastern Nigeria.
We were having tea in the humid leisure of late afternoon, and the Canadian mission doctor was filling in
eleven years for me. I had known Uburu in the
earlier days of make-do-and-mend—the hurricane
lantern held high over the operating-table when the
generator failed, the shuffling queues for 'sewing
medicine' as they called injections, the mixture of
guess and grace that guided a raw young medico among
the diseases of Africa.

Most of the buildings were makeshift then, red
mud-block with dusty roofs of grass. Now the whole
place was trim and well built: wards and surgical
theatre, tidy kitchens, laundry, workshop and general
store. Stiff rows of scarlet canna lilies marked off the
village for men and the village for women and the
church for everyone. All the Africans in the wards
and in the villages and on the yam farms and the
eighty children in the school had one thing in common.
Every one of them was a leper.

All the time I was listening I had my eye on the other
man who was at tea with us. He was quiet in all his
ways—a man who had lived much alone and had
learned to be content with himself. Every now and
then he helped himself from a box of dates and licked
his sticky fingers. The dates were an imported luxury
and a change from the Ibo cook's tea-time inventions.
But what was he doing with the stones? Instead of
leaving them by the side of the plate, tinker-tailor-
soldier-sailor fashion, he was slipping them into his
pocket. Then he would reach out almost absent-

mindedly for another date or two, and sure enough, into his pocket went the stones. Rather messy, I thought, and a bit tropical peculiar.

His name was John Paterson. He was not a doctor or a preacher or a teacher, but a man who made things grow. A very quiet man, but there was hardly a place in that part of Nigeria which could not speak for him. There were the trees he had planted for fruit or shade, the plots he had sown, the birds, beasts and fishes he had brought there. All unmistakably spelled out his handiwork. You could tell that John Paterson had passed that way.

I travelled with him next morning and saw some of it with my own eyes. The dust road was built up above swamps on either side, and we made good speed for an hour on end. I saw men and women wading among thin spears of the brightest green. John Paterson nodded and said just one word: 'Rice'. There had been no rice there when I first knew that country. Now there were acres of it—miles of it.

The rice sells in the traditional markets of the Nigerian villages. It also forms part of the diet in the leprosy settlements. Lepers need not only skilled medical treatment to make them well. Every bit as important is good food, full of proteins and vitamins to build up strong bodies. Leper children recover quickly under treatment, but they must be well fed. They need food that will make them laugh and sing and stand on their hands and turn cart-wheels and win football matches. That was John Paterson's job: to make things grow to make people well.

He began many years ago with a nursery of a thousand oil palms for planting out at Uburu, and quick-growing trees for firewood, as well as oranges, limes, grapefruit and bananas for the leper villages. He tried out a new kind of maize and soya bean to

make porridge for sickly babies. Half the children
born in the villages along the Cross River died before
they were five, killed by malnutrition more often than
by tropical disease. This Scot made porridge to
build healthy and bonny babies. All the same, he
had to admit that his biggest problem was to make
soya taste good.

Fruit is far from common in the African forest,
whatever the story-books may suggest. It has to be
planted and tended, and the strain improved. John
Paterson started a nursery of pineapples and gave away
the suckers to be planted in every school garden in the
district. A new fruit altogether was the carissa
cherry. He set out a bed of cherry stones, then he
carefully dug up the young trees and put each in a
plastic bag so that the roots were not broken or dried
off. At every school he visited he popped in a few
trees and told the children how to look after them.
More than a thousand trees were set out. That means
bright cherries rich in vitamins to pluck and eat on the
way home from school, and free for all.

So that was what the date stones were for. Sure
enough, when we went over the wide Cross River by
pontoon ferry and came to John Paterson's home in
the forest, the first thing he did was to feel in his pocket.
Out came the grubby handful of date stones. One by
one he set them carefully in pots made of hollow bits
of bamboo. No doubt they are growing now in some
school yard or leper village with watchful toddlers on
guard to chase away the goats.

He went out to Africa as a mission carpenter forty-
six years ago, and in his time he has been builder,
engineer road-maker, digger of wells. During the
1939-45 war, when self-support was vital, he was
seconded to the government agricultural department.
That was when rice began to spread an emerald carpet

over Ogoja Province.   He worked in the open lands of
East Africa for a bit; but Nigeria drew him back, to
find himself a post as leprosy supervisor at Yakurr in
the rain forest.   He built his own house there and saw
to the siting and building of the temporary houses for
patients who came in from the riverside villages.

He could turn his hand to anything, this quiet Scot
who spent his days among the lepers.   Birds, beasts
and fishes, all could be helped to grow bigger and
fatter.   A poultry farm to produce a plumper bird
than the usual scrawny African cooking-pot cockerel:
that was a headache for a while, because the two
African girls who carried the balanced chicken feed to
the fowl house found that it was tasty indeed—'sweet
too much', as they would say.   They shared it with
their friends and grew sleek while the chickens starved.
Another experiment was the meadow laid out to feed a
flock of sheep.   And one day all the reasonably fit
lepers were turned out to make a clearing in the
forest.   Their working song improvised comments on
the white man's latest ploy, while their cutlasses made
short work of the tangle of creepers.   That was the
first stage in making a reservoir and a fish farm.
Instead of haggling for a morsel of dried smoked fish
in the market, a leper patient can go fishing in the
fishpond any day he likes, and cook his fresh catch and
eat it for supper.

Everything John Paterson grew he gave away.   All
round him were the leper patients, men and women,
boys and girls, most of them getting better every day.
Almost unnoticed in their midst was the quiet Scot
with his fruit trees and pineapples, his beans, his
beasts and his fishes.   Then the Biafran war came, and
near the end he was compelled to leave.   It is not
likely he will see his African crops again; but they will
aye be growing.

Gleanings from Sheep Street

If every man confined his observations to subjects on which he was qualified to speak, there would be throughout the world a deathly silence—*Chinese proverb*. How warm is the friendship engendered by correspondence—*Ellery Sedgwick*

IS the spring or autumn of the year the best time to enjoy the border country of Wales? I found no cause to contest my host's preference for mist and soft sunlight as we cruised in mid October on the Brecon and Abergavenny canal. The occasion was the re-opening of the waterway by the Secretary of State, who recalled a similar gathering at the first opening in 1800, twelve years before its completion. It now runs for thirty-three miles through the Brecon Beacons National Park to Pontypool, and for twenty-three of them it is lock-free as it winds, often through woods, along the 350-ft contour. In its heyday the canal was used, with tramway feeders, to carry iron, lime and farm produce, but nearly forty years have elapsed since the last toll was taken. Restoration for cruising has been a costly business for British Waterways, even with help from two county councils, who were assisted in turn from national funds on the recommendation of the Countryside Commission. All will continue to share operating and maintenance costs, which will be only partly offset by income from users. How can this most attractive of waterways be made more nearly to pay its way? On that possibility may depend the future of others which could be rehabilitated by similar co-operation between national and local bodies, official and voluntary. The boat club based at Govilon has increased its membership from a handful of enthusiasts to 175 in seven years and has a waiting list for moorings. The annual cost of keeping a 20-ft outboard cruiser on the canal is about £32, including compulsory insurance. There are several slipways for boats brought by road, and two fleets available for holiday hire. If you are ready to be enticed, write to British Waterways at Melbury House, London, N.W.1, for their cruising map and guide.

*

Earlier in the year (Spring, p. 13) we published an article by James Butterfield on the refurbishing of the historic quay at Morwellham on the river Tamar. In twelve weeks after the opening in July it was visited by more than 35,000 people. Another enterprising venture is the Weald and Downland Open Air Museum near the village of Singleton in West Sussex. It has been fortunate in its sponsors and its director, John Lowe, who was previously at the Victoria and Albert and Birmingham museums. Buildings which could no longer remain on their original sites—one would have been destroyed by a reservoir, another by a road improvement—are being re-erected on an attractive stretch of meadow backed by trees. They include a fourteenth-century Kentish farmhouse, a Wealden hall, two granaries, an Elizabethan treadwheel in its own thatched building from Hampshire, and a toll house from Upper Beeding in Sussex. Volunteers, including police cadets, have worked hard on the site and buildings; and the re-erection of a granary from Littlehampton was sponsored by the Round Table there. There is space for picnicking, and at the end of a pleasant woodland walk I found a charcoal-turner's hut, kiln and oven. A dozen miles away in Hampshire plans are afoot for an iron-age farm on Butser Hill, and possibly a Romano-British one— further pointers for providers of country parks.

*

'Ellum she hateth man', we say, when the most characteristic of our hedgerow trees drops a branch.

In fact, both beech and horse chestnut are more dangerous. The point was made at a meeting called by the Forestry Commission to discuss the present epidemic of 'Dutch' elm disease, so named because more research has been done on it in the Netherlands than elsewhere. It has been endemic in Britain for some forty years, occasionally flaring up, but quiescent for some time until the upsurge which began three years ago. The fungus, which is carried by the elm bark beetle, usually attacks at the junction of a twig with a larger branch. The vessels in the wood then become blocked, and the supply of nutrients to the leaves is gradually impeded or cut off, until the diagnostic bare boughs and others with prematurely sere foliage make their appearance. Sometimes the tree dies; sometimes it recovers, or the infection does not spread. The control measures suggested in the Commission's Research and Development Paper, 'The Dying Elms', are the felling of all trees with dead or half-dead crowns, the burning of branch-wood on site and the stripping of bark from trees awaiting removal. Fortunately the value of the timber is not affected by the disease, and in especially hard-hit areas—parts of the West Midlands, Kent, Essex and south-east Hampshire—the Commission advises groups of owners to combine operations, thus improving their chances of selling the trees to a contractor and increasing effective control. The research programme has been stepped up, but no practicable method of chemical or biological control has yet been found. There has been speculation recently about an 'Austrian wasp'— in fact, an ichneumonid—which parasitises the larva of the beetle. The introduction of the more resistant commelin elm from Holland has also been suggested; but it has a habit different from that of our own elm, which to many people is almost the hallmark of the traditional English landscape. There may be some correlation between fine summers and outbreaks of the disease; as J. S. R. Chard pointed out, we have had two good seasons for butterflies, and probably for beetles too. If next summer is a wet one, it may at least suit our remaining elms.

*

Readers who came to know Raymond Bush as a warm-hearted and knowledgeable friend through his 'Fruit Grower's Diary' often ask for news of him. At eighty-five, with arthritis in both knees, he writes, 'I have to do most of my gardening sitting in a chair; but it is surprising what can be managed with a flat hoe with a 10-ft handle. I have just left my recently planted tomato patch as clean as a whistle, and not a weed will survive the 120° F. Jamaican sun. Seedlings are no problem, and I can sit and mix my soil and fill trays to my heart's content. Occasionally I do a little hibiscus grafting or take cuttings. In the twenty years I have been in Jamaica, almost everything in my garden, from palm trees downwards, has been grown from seeds or cuttings filched from my friends.

'There are occasional problems. Some years ago, on the rocky slope below my house where I had built a bungalow in 1957, I planted a few ponciana trees, which are clothed in scarlet bloom for a month. One, between the bungalow and my veranda, grew too big and I had to pollard it every year, cutting the growth right back to the main stem. Later I decided I would let it flower. It grew enormously; but in the second year, when the flower buds began to come out in June, I saw to my horror that every cluster was crawling with massive black beetles. These had hatched from the larvae of the dung-beetles which infest the droppings from my neighbour's cattle. Normally the beetles spread far and wide in their feeding, but my ponciana happened to bloom early and so got the full force of the attack, which heavy spraying failed to control. Soon after, the bungalow toilet-bowl split and tiles began to cascade from the bathroom walls. My ponciana had managed to push a root through the concrete foundation and under the floor tiles, so to my regret I had to cut it down. In ten years the trunk had reached a circumference of more than 3 ft. My pride and joy at present is a parasitic vine which grew from a small cutting in 1952 and has now made a top 30 ft across and 20 ft thick on a large cedar stump. Ten years ago it started to bloom, and I identified it as a red-hot poker tree. Now the 8-ft shoots carry up to eight vermilion flower-heads apiece, and the middle of the tree looks like a house on fire. Two years ago a miniature whirlwind whistled down on to it and snatched up about a quarter of the vine, with a 40-lb. piece of the cedar stump, dropping it some yards away. Then it whizzed down to a tall coconut palm and tied one long leaf into a knot.

'I can crop small melons at any time of year, but not these nor all the mangoes, pawpaws, bananas, oranges and grapefruits can make up for the strawberries, raspberries, peaches, plums and apples that I used to grow in England. I miss them still.'

*

I have nothing to add to Stephen Dalton's admirably helpful report on this year's photographic competition which appears on p. 273. In view of the high standard achieved, we have decided to run the competition again next year with the theme, 'Life in a Village'. The judge will be Louis F. Peek, whose book 'Cash from Your Camera' was reviewed in the Autumn Number (p. 146). The rules are on p. 416.—*J. C.*

PENETRATING THE FUTURE
by Tom Parker

Near Straiton, Ayrshire: fertilising young spruce

and mid-morning break, by William S. Paton

THE TRAVELLER
by John Keene

A Fruit Grower Looks Back—2
by D. Macer Wright

ON a misty November morning we bade farewell to Surrey and headed west. I was to take up a roving commission in field work—from Cheshire, which is about the northerly limit of English fruit farming, to the south coast. Basically my concern was orchard pest and disease control, but I soon became involved in the many other activities which field work embraces.

I had come from an area of rainfall ideal for fruit growing and had experience of only two primary soil types. It was revealing to work in regions where the rainfall averaged some 15 in. above that I had previously known, and where soils varied from Cotswold limestone and Pershore clay to hot sandstones without marl of the Ross-on-Wye series, the deep sandstones with marl around Bromyard and the rich red earths of Devonshire. In Berkshire there was soil that looked like porridge, yet grew magnificent cherries; on the Hampshire greensands I was much at home, but one orchard just off the fringe of the New Forest was on sticky clay and needed a full-scale drainage scheme.

My introduction to this land of contrasts was on a decidedly glum note. The new low-volume spraying system, using a fine mist of micronised droplets, would, I was assured, be hopeless in the west. 'You've never seen our scab', they said. In fact I had, but that seemed to brand me as a dangerous lunatic rather than a harmless crank. Nowhere, not even around Wisbech in Cambridgeshire, is scab more devastating than in the west. It can make unsprayed apples look like boiler fuel.

After following some initial trials, a few brave

The author's first article under this heading appeared in Summer 1970, p. 245.

spirits launched into the new method. It was firmly established in the Kentish Weald, where conditions were not so different from those in Herefordshire. It was also defeating the Wisbech scab; and in Essex, where red-spider mite was the great problem, it had become accepted by leading growers. But most of the venturesome were of the modern generation, new to fruit farming, who had opted for the open air instead of city desks. The old hands were less ready to back the backroom boys. In the West Country a native caution has informed fruit growing throughout its long history. They like to watch and wait, to see whether the new-fangled ways succeed or fail, which is easy enough these days when growers from all parts visit each other's farms.

Shortly after the new pioneers had trailed their toys round the orchard, a lecturer said that, if anyone had bought a low-volume sprayer, he might as well dig a hole and bury it: at £600, an expensive hole. But the virtues of the system became evident as time passed, and the 'scab year' for which I was waiting soon came; such a year is never absent for long in the west. I had some half dozen trials scattered over the region, and at the season's end every one showed that low-volume had confounded its critics. Gradually it spread, and I doubt whether there is now a grower with a sizable orchard anywhere who has not long since adopted some form of it. The fixed boom hydraulic sprayer, gushing out its three or four hundred gallons of dilute wash per acre, is now little more than a mechanised brontosaurus, as outdated as the horse-drawn barrel with high rig that first started all the fuss nearly a hundred years ago.

Much of my work consisted of testing new spray materials and assessing their impact on pests, diseases and predators, speed and degree of control, phytotoxic

effects (if any), possibilities of damage to fruit and like
questions. Sometimes assessments had to be related
to individual problems of soil, local climate, nutrient
status of the trees and methods of spray application.
I do not know whether I taught anybody anything,
but I learned a great deal.

I learned, for example, how faith in one's experience, in the face of prophecies of doom, can save time
and money. On a farm in Somerset where the land
was deep and moist, the sward green with nature's
chlorophyll, owing nothing to nitro-chalk, and where
no red-spider spray had been given in the fifteen
years of the orchard's life, mites appeared suddenly on
an outside row. They multiplied visibly, and a
chemical salesman told the grower that if no spray
were applied, the orchard would become smothered.
The grower, as he put it, dithered and dithered, half
sure of himself, half afraid the salesman was right.
He got to the point of lifting up the telephone to order
some bugwash, then said to himself, 'No, I'm hanged
if I will. I'll give them a few more days'. Within a
week the mites had diminished. After ten days they
had all but vanished, gobbled up by the predators
that abounded on trees which had never known DDT
or parathion.

But every coin has two sides. In commercial fruit
growing, where certain afflictions can spread through
hundreds of trees within short periods, it is vital to
know your pests and diseases, to be able to forecast
the probable turn of events, and to be ever ready to
apply preventive measures where necessary. One
farmer had recently bought a dairy farm to which
were attached a few acres of Bramleys, Newtons and
other cookers. He rang me up one May evening to
say that frost had killed every blossom, and that he
had just heard from the locals that it had struck nearly

every season for years past.   Fewer than ten minutes were needed to discover that the 'frost' was apple sucker.   I had not seen such an infestation; it reminded me of tales my grandfather used to tell of 'blight' on Vale of Evesham plums before the advent of tar-oil. The following winter the farmer applied tar-oil, and the next summer the trees were laden with apples. The locals could hardly believe their eyes.

In those pre-myxomatosis days rabbits were still a perennial enemy of young trees, and dozens of growers were engaged on new plantings.   Few things in the orchard are so depressing as tree stems stripped of bark; it means either replacement or the long and tedious job of bridge-grafting.   Boundary netting was expensive and its erection time-consuming, though it was really the only effective answer and had to be done before planting.   Stem cages are of limited use on bush trees, since rabbits can usually surmount them, the cage top acting as a foot-rest while the animal eats its fill.

In some orchards whole rows of young trees would be attacked.   An efficient repellent was sorely needed. I had various trials in progress, some with stuff having a smell that would stop an elephant, but not rabbits. Eventually something with a mild aroma was found to work, much to the relief of my wife, who was seriously thinking of casting around for an old gas-mask.   A less loyal spouse might have sought a separation on grounds of atmospheric pollution.

Field work teaches the danger of assuming that a particular set of rules always has universal application. Fresh from reasonable success with dwarf pyramids, I was sorry to find that, in the west, the system had brought endless difficulties and had got itself a bad name.   Many plots had become jungles; others had been thinned to leave that unfortunate half-way state

where the remaining trees are too close for open-plan
culture, and too wide to exert the root restriction
needed to tame shoot growth.   Others again had been
thinned to open plans, which is the only way; but it
needs the strongest will-power, since to a plant of,
say, 8 ft by 3 ft, the nearest true open plan is 16 ft by
12 ft, which means taking out almost 1600 trees from
each acre.   They make a very large funeral pyre, if
there is no spare land to take them; and even if there
is, their transplanting and staking can put paid to any
preconceived seasonal programme.

During the inter-war years the belief became
established that for Cox's as a pyramid, M II was the
ideal stock.   So it was, on light land; but on the deep
West Country soils it could be disastrous, and M VII
or even M IX would have given a totally different
picture.

I found one splendid plot on the foothills of the
Quantocks, where the grower had used his own good
judgement over rootstocks, instead of accepting advice
founded on quite different conditions of soil and local
climate.   It was a joy to see those trees, neat, correctly
shaped and carrying the heaviest crops the method
then allowed.   As I had been a strong advocate of the
pyramid, I felt that my belief in its value, where rootstocks and varieties were correctly related to soil, was
fully vindicated.

Another thing which field work carried out over an
extensive area teaches is that to the fruit grower the
term 'local climate' can mean much more than is
conveyed by television weather charts, excellent though
these are.   Over a certain narrow belt of Herefordshire, perhaps no more than half a mile wide,
hailstorms—short, sharp, but severe—frequently occur
as an annual feature.   There may be only one each
summer, but the hailstones can be large enough to

damage an apple crop to the point where it is down graded by 6d or more per lb. Yet orchards on either side of this belt will escape.

Then there is an area just below the western escarpment of the north Cotswolds which may go for weeks without rain, while rain will be seen teeming down all about the surrounding countryside.

Soil too can vary astonishingly even on the same farm. I recall an orchard of fine apple and pear trees in land that was pretty well self-supporting. The adjacent field, only a hedgerow away, was planted to gooseberries one autumn. The following summer they showed the most complete signs of potassium deficiency—so bad that fertiliser dressings were of no avail and the whole lot had to be ploughed in.

Devonshire is, of course, renowned for its deep soil, but it also has greensand areas of a particularly hungry kind. On one of these a mixed orchard, grown organically, was struggling hard and without much success for lack of adequate manure. It was a classic case of spreading too thinly. There was not enough material to cover the whole plantation sufficiently, and it never went on at more than 10 tons per acre, usually less. Before it could build up fertility and conserve water, it burnt itself out. On hot land, and when organics are scarce, there is only one thing to do: rotate the manure at 20 tons per acre and keep the trees on the undressed areas going with foliar sprays, plus fertilisers if necessary.

Several times I came across this insistence on organics only, in circumstances where the orchard was praying for a sensible compromise. It is faith of the most irrational kind—faith made dogma.

To cover all the aspects of fruit farming with which I came into contact in those six years would be impossible here. Suffice it to say that after motoring some 200,000 miles, seeing a great deal of an England that was and still is very beautiful in spite of the valiant efforts of planners to bury it all under concrete, and after sleeping in far too many beds, I found myself pining for an anchorage once again within the boundaries of a home orchard. There really is nothing like stepping out of your back door straight into apple blossom.

Culture on Wheels
by H. F. Ellis

'IT'S the mobile today, don't forget.' Culture of a kind, certainly; though not of the kind that sprouts extensions from itself, like metal strawberry runners, and rotates in intricate convolutions about eccentric foci. The 'mobile', only a dedicated townsman will need to be told, is our travelling library, bringing a fortnightly benison of books to the village and announcing its arrival with a loud summons on its hooter.

Every other Wednesday, at twenty to four, the mobile parks outside the post office (and stores) on a bit of a hill. It is exceedingly well sprung, reacting instantly to the arrival of a new customer, and the combination of this up-and-down movement with the slope of the floor produces the sensation of being at sea on a choppy day. This alone makes it more interesting than any borough library. Some of us, after five minutes on deck in a crouching position with the head held at the angle required to read the titles on the

lowest shelves (or scuppers), have to go outside for a
breath of air.

The number of books the mobile can accommodate
on its shelves is considerable, but finite. One is not
baffled and depressed by the sheer multiplicity of
choice, as in more static libraries where the fiction
section alone may have three or four shelves devoted to
authors beginning with 'W'. A certain freedom to
pick and choose is pleasant; one would not want to
live in a country where the choice is between 'Mao's
Thoughts' and nothing. But there is a point at which
the mind is shackled rather than set free by variety;
and not only in the matter of books. A nurseryman's
catalogue that I have before me lists, on a quick count,
386 different heath and heather cultivars. How can
I pick the dozen and a half for which I have room
from that lot, especially when I am told in the cultural
instructions not to plant in groups of less than six to a
dozen of each? At best I am going to end up with 383
kinds unrepresented in my garden. Another firm, I
believe, offers more than 600 varieties of fuchsia.
This must be almost as stultifying to fuchsia-lovers as
it is for suit-buyers to be asked by their tailors to thumb
through six great wodges of cloth samples, each
containing over fifty patterns ranging from dark grey
to near-black. Human discrimination has its limits.

The mobile, as I was saying, avoids this oppressive
catholicity. Disregarding books already read, the
children's section and a rather too specialised little
group about wireless telegraphy and the maintenance
of motor-cycle engines, what remains poses no impossible problem of selection. And the mobile pos-
sesses a further advantage: half an hour to the minute
after the hooter has announced its arrival it will be
moving off again, so a term is set to the customer's
indecision. The pressure thus exerted, reinforced

on occasion by a touch of seasickness, often leads to the choice of a book one would not conceivably take from less transient shelves. This broadens the mind.

I would not ordinarily take the Duke of Cumberland home as a companion through the long winter evenings. One might as well pick Addington—as I did not long

ago, thanks to the mobile, and very soon learned how wrong I had been to dismiss the poor old chap as both dull and incompetent. This one, called 'The Damnable Duke of Cumberland', is an even more thoroughgoing vindication, rising to considerable heights of indignation on behalf of this worthy and misunderstood man who ought never to have been accused of murder, rape and incest. The great thing about vindications is that authors, in pursuit of a pious determination to rehabilitate their maligned heroes, can cut loose against a whole battalion of damnable traducers—including, in this case, Greville, Creevey, the Princess Lieven (perhaps), an anonymous contributor to the 'New Statesman' of a date in March 1963 and a bevy of unprincipled Whigs. I have never yet read a vindication without feeling that a revindication of all the people who came so badly out of it was now a crying literary need.

Socially the mobile is a great asset. It seems to be inevitable in any village that there should be some half dozen people whose names simply do not stick in the mind. More accurately, their names stick, but which name belongs to which remains a mystery. They would not look particularly alike if ranged together at an identification parade but, seen separately, some common quality of build or (as with tailors' patterns) greyness or, it may be, of wicker basket on their bicycles seems to predominate. So it is, at any rate, for me.

The mobile librarian never hesitates. 'Good afternoon, Mrs Ingleby', he calls from behind his little counter as she mounts the steps; and I, crouching among the biographies at the farther end, blush to think that, after five years' residence in the village, I am so easily shamed by this half-an-hour-a-fortnight visitor. But at least I can get it right this time, and need only wait until the lady gravitates downhill towards me before greeting her with a confident 'Hello, Mrs Ingleby'. With any luck she will now believe that the person who hailed her as Miss Tremayne at our last three meetings in the post office must have been somebody else. After all, I may be one of her half dozen grey indistinguishables.

The librarian, a man of remarkable calibre, remembers tastes as well as names. This is an invaluable gift when we are, as often happens, taking in each other's washing. Those who are unable, for one reason or another, to keep the fortnightly tryst naturally ask a neighbour to return the books they last took out and 'bring me one or two more'. In requesting this small service they are not always very helpful about the kind of thing they like to read. 'I don't much care for those cruel things' may be the sole guidance one gets. Nor, if some less negative preference is expressed, can the obliging neighbour be entirely certain that it is not coloured by a little harmless snobbery. It is one thing to whip a couple of S. F. novels off the shelves, slip a life of Nelson on top and put the small pile down quietly on the librarian's counter; it is quite another to come right out into the open with Miss Palfrey and tell her that something interplanetary is required. The librarian cuts clean through these mists of reticence or incoherence.

'For Mr Cantling?' he will say. 'There's an Ambler just come back that I don't think he's had.'

Thus we all get what we want without loss of status; for Mr Cantling, if he wishes, can disown the librarian's insight with a humorous raising of the eyebrows and a 'Well, well, I suppose I must dip into it'.

The treasures the mobile displays on its shelves are, of course, no more than its shop window. Behind it lie the unplumbed resources of the county library; and you have only to ask for a particular title—preferably getting it nearly right and adding the author's name, if known—to have it waiting there for you a fortnight later. Free, friendly and efficient, the mobile library supplies a service the village would be lost without.

There goes the hooter. Who knows what mind-broadening volume I shall return with in half an hour's time?

YORKSHIREMAN who, after playing the French horn in village band for many years, moved to town and joined the band there: 'Nowt to it. They only let me blow when t' conductor wags 'is stick at me. Back in t' village Ah played ivery note fra start ti finish'.

As a Farmer Sees It
by Tristram Beresford

AN excellent lamb crop, a continental summer, an insatiable demand for straw at £1 an acre behind the combines: these have been the high spots of the year at Chilmark. Our winter wheat was a comfort when spring-sown barley and beans yellowed off in May and stayed yellow in June: just as well that we had a hundred acres of it; it was the only cereal that yielded above average this season. For the first time in our lives we were all set to make prime hay, having adapted a dutch barn for warm-air blowing and laid in the equipment to blow with. But the halcyon weeks of early summer, so inviting to bask in, gave us dwarf crops of hay as well as dwarf crops of beans and barley; and, like most people, we were short of grass until August. The corn harvest, though disappointing, had this to be said for it: it was easy and early. Crops were dry and standing, and the weather was adequate, so we romped through them in continental style. In north-east France, where they can count on dry seasons in four years out of five, they normally get outputs of five tons an hour from a 10-ft combine. They simply use a higher gear than we do. This year conditions were right for us too, and we were able to keep up with them. In spite of mechanical breakdowns we harvested 500 acres in little more than three weeks—usually it is five and a half—and as soon as we were out of a field, the contractor was in, baling up the wakes and loading away. However, in the final reckoning, cereal output was down 6 cwt an acre on 1969. Our other main enterprise, eggs, has had a thin time, too: price down 2d a dozen, and yield per bird down a bit as well. With feed prices rising because of the maize and barley famine, and a continuing surplus of eggs on the home market, the further outlook is unsettled. Needless to add, we get no relief, as poultry farmers, from Mr Prior's autumn hand-out.

'It's all right for you arable farmers,' said a fertiliser manufacturer, 'look at the prices you're getting for wheat and barley.   You've made a killing, and you'll be spreading artificials an inch thick next year'.   This statement, offered as a serious comment and coming from a man who prides himself on being inside the agricultural family, is remarkable for the ignorance it reveals about the way our support system works.   It has to be taken seriously, because if a great ancillary trade can get it as wrong as that, what must the general public think?   The truth is that cereal growers as a whole will benefit not at all from the scarcity prices on the grain market this autumn: deficiency payments will be lower, that is all; and perhaps, for barley, there may not even be one.   What happened was that the market was under-supplied and therefore strong enough to return virtually the whole of the government-guaranteed price to the farmer, leaving the Treasury with a windfall of £60m. or so at the expense of the livestock industry.   To be sure, some of this windfall has been pledged in higher guarantees.   But for the average arable farmer the gross return on cereals from the 1970 harvest will be little better than it was last year.   Individuals who jumped in at the right moment have reason to be pleased with their judgment, or their luck; others, who sold ahead before the boom, will wear long faces for months to come.   Ourselves, at Chilmark, we expect to make the guaranteed price, no more.   We might have done better with the wisdom of hindsight.   And we might have done worse.

We can see now, looking back, that the stage was set for a grain boom this autumn.   In northern Europe spring was cold and late, summer fine and warm. Weather affected not only our home barley crop, but the French crop as well. In E.E.C. as a whole the grain harvest, excluding maize and rice, was said to be lighter than usual. Then came news of leaf blight in the U.S. maize crop. It was rumoured that the whole of the anticipated surplus—10m. tons as a rule—had been wiped out by fungus disease. This was enough to cause the biggest trading spree on the Chicago grain futures market in all its 122 years of history. In London, Mark Lane took fright at once. Maltsters scrambled to buy samples they would never look at in normal circumstances, and what they rejected was exported to Germany for malting there. The seed and feed trades were caught in the updraught; and high freight rates and pessimistic estimates of the domestic barley crop kept prices buoyant. Although, as I write, the American crop is claimed to be 5m. tons better than was thought at first, and France—she lies low and says nothing—probably has a bumper crop of maize under the counter, there seems little prospect of the boom subsiding. This, in a nutshell, is why it has been a harvest of trouble for consumers in Britain: dearer bread, dearer meat, dearer confectionery, dearer milk and dearer beer—and all because of our vulnerability as a nation which has to import 8m. tons of grain a year, half of it for animal feed.

One's first impulse is to say: don't let us be caught another time. Let us be self-sufficient in future. But on closer inspection this argument falls down. About half our imports are of hard wheat, which our climate does not allow us to grow, and for which—public taste in bread being what it is—it is impossible to substitute more than a certain amount of home-grown grain. It is our maize and barley imports that make us vulnerable to fluctuations in supply, and since we have not found a maize to suit us, the best we can do is to substitute barley and oats for some of our maize imports. This is what agriculture's little Neddy recommended in 1968, though the committee argued the case for more wheat as well, chiefly for animal feed. What has become apparent since then is that the steam has gone out of agricultural technology. As Stuart Wragg has shown, advances in yield that it seemed reasonable to expect five years ago have not been realised. The years of affluence and expansion are over. The growth-rate has slowed down. We have reached a plateau, and the cost of equipping the industry for another great leap forward now seems exorbitant. This, anyway, is the main argument for not insuring against an occasional grain famine. But there is another argument too: under any system of price support for agriculture, a small excess of production can be as expensive as a small deficiency. If the weather had not been exceptional, world grain yields would have been normal instead of abnormal, and we would have had a million tons too much barley instead of a million tons too little. In that event cereal deficiency payments would have cost the Exchequer a lot more than the £73m. estimated in this year's White Paper.

It was at Michaelmas 1949 that we moved from Manor Farm, Fitzhead, to Manor Farm, Chilmark. To be precise, it was on October 3rd that the first lorry-loads of live and deadstock turned in here; and the movement went on, as I remember, for four days, involving 51 journeys, not counting the tractors and laden trailers that did the trip by road. At our farm supper this year we celebrated our twenty-first anniversary at Chilmark, and looked back over a period covering almost two-thirds of our lives as occupiers of agricultural land. From the beginning we kept records—at first too many, and latterly no more than we strictly need to keep. Looking through them, we can say that the first seven years at Chilmark were a time of consolidation, of finding our feet on one and a half square miles of thin chalk after years of vegetation in the kindlier soils of the Vale of Taunton Deane. It was a time of trial and error: sugar beet, potatoes and other cash crops we had been used to were tried out and discarded. The dairy herd, which promised well in Somerset, proved to be a wasting asset and had to go. There were couch-grass and wild oats to be dealt with too. The abuses of war-time cropping had to be rectified, fertility restored, and each field studied and coaxed in the direction we wished to take. So it is only in the last fourteen years or so that our records have become meaningful as a series; and it was these I drew on at our farm supper this autumn to illustrate the progress we have made together, because some of the original members of the farm staff were there, those who are still working and those who have retired. I find, for instance, that we produce about double the tonnage of grain we produced in 1957, more than double the quantity of eggs and more than treble the number of lambs. Cereal yields, on a four-year moving average, have risen from 29 cwt an acre to just under 35 cwt in spite of a 25 per cent increase in cereal acreage; but it is worth noting that we have been on the plateau of 35 cwt, give or take a hundredweight or two, since the early sixties. Egg yields too have reached their ceiling at around 280 eggs a bird, on a hen-day reckoning, and so has our lambing rate at 175 per cent. From first-hand experience, therefore, we support the Wragg thesis: we have had our burst of energy and are now expending all our efforts to stay in the same position. This is not as easy as it sounds. In terms of turnover, the return we get today for all we produce—in spite of doubling or trebling our physical output—is only just 3 per cent more, in real terms, than it was fifteen years ago.

Net income, of course, has fallen.   It is all we can do, after
salaries,   dividends,   corporation   tax,   shortfall   liability,
income tax and surtax, to maintain the real value of our
assets; and if inflation goes on at its present rate, that task
too will be beyond us.   The one positive gain registered in
our records is the rise in purchasing power of weekly-paid
wages. These, in actual terms, have gone up two and a
half times since 1957, and in real terms by two-thirds.

One conference I did not go to this summer was a meeting
convened in Paris to discuss the problems of marginal
farming in E.E.C.   I almost went.   In fact, I got as far as
a small hotel in the valley of the Loir, intending to com-
mute from there.   But having studied the documentation,
which was copious and closely reasoned, I decided to play
truant, not only because the petunias were in flower, but
also because the older I get, the less capable do I feel of
making a contribution to a discussion between experts.
Moreover it was the weekend of the Quatorze Juillet when,
on the whole, people tend not to work in France from about
Thursday until the following Wednesday morning.   So
instead of going to Paris, as I had been graciously invited
to do, I headed south to the Massif Central, which is one
of the most marginal areas in the whole of French agriculture.   There were four million Frenchmen on the road,
but I did not meet any, because I went by the *petites routes
d'écolier* and these, as in England, are shunned by holiday-
makers hurtling to the sea.   In the Parc des Volcans and
in the high country round the Puy de Sancy there were the
usual trippers and campers from Clermont Ferrand.   But
the life of the countryside went on in spite of them, at its
own deliberate pace—haymaking, cows being driven into
the byres to be milked, and the pasturing of flocks of sheep,
with grandmother in attendance, knitting.   Many of

these farms run a tractor now—second-hand, probably, but sufficient.   There was time to stop and talk, farmer to farmer, in the bright sunshine; and if I had a critical observation, it was that most of the country people were middle-aged or older.   A whole generation was missing. I did not find any problems.

But this, of course, is the core of the problem: the missing generation—the young who are missing from these areas because they are condemned to miss so much that life can offer, if they remain in them.   We have the same pheno- menon in Britain.   When we gave up our hill farm in the Upper Towy valley, our shepherd's family were the only children of school age in an area of 500 square miles. Get up early in County Fermanagh or County Tyrone, and what do you see?   The girls from the farms in their smartest wear, waiting for the bus to take them to their jobs in town.   In the Mezzogiorno the so-called economic miracle in the north of Italy has exerted so powerful a pull on youth that only the dying are left behind on the land. And there you have the problem in its final stage, because all vitality has been drained away, life has retreated into the shadows of doorways, and in the villages you find a glum resentment against all intruders.   But where the process of social denudation is not so far advanced in the Kaisergebirge, for instance, or in the Higher Engadine where the ghost of Lou von Salomé still walks, or even in Wengen out of season where the absence of the internal combustion engine is nothing short of deafening, these semi-depleted rural zones offer something for which the whole privileged urban world, the unceasing stream of people on the move, are searching—peace, the sacred vanishing commodity, peace.   That is the paradox. These problem areas of modern agriculture still have it, for just so long as change holds off, and the elderly, having so little and yet so much, hold on. Is there no social amber in which they can be preserved, they and their kind, for the sake of their benign and mellow influence?

Welsh Ways

IN our Denbighshire village there is a wedding custom known as 'Saving a Good Man'. It consists simply in waiting until the bridegroom arrives at the church and then blocking every approach road but one, so that the bride is delayed and the groom has a chance of second thoughts. Carts and hurdles used to form the road blocks; today it is tractors. As far as I can tell, it happens only when both bride and groom are from the parish or from near by. The last occasion was some five years ago, and the bride had to make a detour of nearly ten miles. Her mother was furious. But there is no record of any bridegroom having taken advantage of his opportunity.

Another local custom, kept up until recently, concerned the delicate matter of fees at funerals. Each member of the bereaved family rose in turn from his seat in church, walked round the coffin and placed a piece of silver on it to pay the parson. At the grave-side they would find two shovels laid crosswise on the path, to remind them that the grave-digger too had earned his fee. Hanging on the west wall of our church is a long-handled six-sided collecting box which, I am told, was used instead of the shovels, or as well, by a former grave-digger of grasping disposition. 'Mean old so-and-so', commented one villager. 'Used to get two pound ten for scything the churchyard twice a year and then went round selling the hay'.—
E. G. Fowler

Birds in Boxes
by Bruce Campbell

> 'So the bluebirds have contracted, have they, for a house?
>   And a nest is under way for little Mr Wren?'
> 'Hush, dear, hush! Be quiet, dear, quiet as a mouse.
>   These are weighty secrets and we must whisper them.'

THIS affecting verse by Susan Coolidge appeared
in 1920 on the title page of a booklet issued by a
Canadian Ministry and called 'Bird Houses and Their
Occupants'. Its sentiments are somewhat distant from
those of the simple European peasants who, certainly
in the sixteenth century and probably much earlier,
began to put up wooden or clay *cistulae* on houses or
trees to attract starlings and sparrows. When the
brood was near fledging, it was removed and supple-
mented the family's meagre diet. Sometimes a
second brood was allowed to fledge; but the clay pots
made at Delft, where sparrows were regarded as a pest
by the brewing industry, were used to control numbers.
It emerged from correspondence in 'British Birds'
some years ago that sparrow and starling pots were
common not only in Silesia, as recorded in a German
journal by Dr Erwin Stresemann, and Flanders, but in
Italy, the French Vosges, where they were called *pots
de moineaux* and in use up to the 1914-18 war, and in
Kent and Sussex up to the middle of the last century.
John Buxton quoted from a poem by Thomas Ran-
dolph (died 1635), who drew a somewhat uncompli-
mentary simile between his mistress's bosom and 'pots
to nest young sparrows in'. Professor Meiklejohn
pointed out that both starlings and flasks can be seen
in Pieter Bruegel's picture of Mad Margaret, and I
have detected them since in several other paintings of
the sixteenth and seventeenth centuries.

A model of a starling flask was shown at the recent International Ornithological Congress at The Hague; presumably the young were shaken out of the neck. The pots in the Vosges were hung from nails and had open backs which fitted tightly against the wall; and flowerpots have been used in the same way by modern birdwatchers.   Starlings and sparrows are small game; wild duck are a much better proposition.   Long baskets made of plaited osiers or straw, used in Holland for many years to attract nesting mallard, are now to be found in wildfowl collections and nature reserves in Britain.   Quite independently, many miles to the north, the Lapps began to farm the palatable eggs of the goldeneye duck, which nests in cavities.   At first they improved natural sites; later came deep nestboxes, now used to encourage breeding and found hopefully round some Scottish lochs.   According to a traveller at the end of the last century, the Lapps summarily ejected smews and owls which took over goldeneye boxes, or sold their skins and eggs to collectors.

The modern demand for Indian hill mynahs as talking pets has given new life to an ancient practice of the Garo tribe in Assam. In their villages B. C. R. Bertram found tapering baskets of split bamboo, about five feet long and a foot wide at the centre, and covered with straw. They are most attractive to the mynahs when strung high between the branches of a tree at an angle of 45°, the entrance hole being about a third of the way from the top end and pointing downwards. The birds are removed when fairly young, fed artificially and then sold for as much as 10s or £1 at the local market.   The device is apparently peculiar to the Garos.

So the Old World ancestors of the nestbox were severely practical in intent; it was the Indians of North America who set European invaders a higher

example. In the 1830s Alexander Wilson described
how the Chactaw and Chickasaw tribes pruned trees
near their camps and, on the prongs of branches, hung
hollowed-out gourds or calabashes for the colonial
purple martin to nest in. John James Audubon,
Wilson's rival, immortalised these gourds in his painting
of the martin, showing a male crouched at the entrance
hole; and he remarked that 'almost every country
tavern has a martin-box on the upper part of its sign-
board, and I have observed that the handsomer the box,
the better does the inn usually prove to be'. He also
said that martins chased away vultures from the Indian
camps, and Wilson wrote that man derived 'considerable advantage as well as amusement' from these birds,
so it is possible that the association with the Indians
was of mutual benefit: there would no doubt be plenty
of flies round the encampments for the martins to
catch. Perhaps their presence was also considered
lucky, like that of swallows on British farms. Not so
long ago a Welsh farmer would not let me ring a
brood in his cowshed in case I frightened them away.

About the time Wilson wrote, Charles Waterton was
making provision for hole-nesting birds on his York-

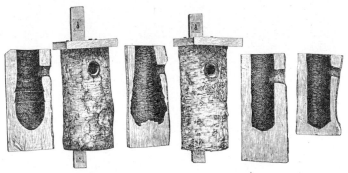

Berlepsch woodpecker box: two on left, 'correct'; others, 'worthless imitations'

shire estate. He is usually credited as the first man to do so with a definite conservation motive, though it was suggested some years ago in 'Countryman Club' that holes or windows in lofts to attract barn owls might have a very long history, because their value as hunters of rats and mice was recognised. To a stone and mortar cavity for barn owls on a ruined gateway, Charles Waterton added two dozen holes for starlings, and eventually nine kinds of bird nested on this ivied ruin. He experimented with sites for duck and made a bank for sand martins with 56 drainpipes as nest holes, going some way to anticipate the ingenious techniques used by modern photographers to get inside shots of hole-nests. He died in 1865. Within twenty-five years what is now the Royal Society for the Protection of Birds had been formed and Britain had its first protective legislation. The wooden nestbox made its appearance in gardens, and by 1897 J. R. B. Masefield knew of twenty species that had used boxes of some design. He also described the attempts of Charles Buxton, M.P., to introduce parrots and cockatoos on his Norfolk estate. Some did use boxes, and grey parrots adopted a litter of kittens in one of them, keeping up 'constant warfare' with the mother cat.

If Charles Waterton was the morning star of bird protection, its Luther was Baron Hans von Berlepsch of Seebach in Thuringia. The baron, to change the human metaphor, found his Boswell in Martin Hiesemann, whose book 'How to Attract and Protect Wild Birds' was published in 1907 and translated next year into English; it reached a third edition in 1912. The protection of birds, according to the baron, 'can only be attained through Nature herself, or through an exact imitation of Nature'. On this principle the only successful nestbox reproduced the woodpecker borings which he was convinced hole-nesting birds preferred to any other cavities. So authoritative was his claim that Berlepsch boxes were manufactured on quite a large scale in Germany and Austria and put up in thousands in state and private forests; he was also paid the compliment of having them pirated by 'unscrupulous tradesmen'. There were three different sizes to the same design, accommodating anything from a coal tit to a tawny owl, a box for swifts which was fixed horizontally with a semi-circular opening at one end, and a small open-fronted type for redstarts, spotted flycatchers, pied wagtails and robins.

The baron was not only concerned to encourage hole-nesting birds for their own sakes. He saw them in a new role, not for consumption by hungry peasants but as valuable consumers themselves. In the spring of 1905 a plague of caterpillars entirely stripped the leaves of a wood not far from Seebach; but the baron's wood, with its 2000 nestboxes, was untouched. 'It stood out among the remaining woods like a green oasis', while a quarter of a mile away, at the limit of the birds' feeding range, 'first traces of the plague were apparent'. The view that sufficient insectivorous birds can control a defoliating pest has been strongly held by many German and other foresters ever since. British research carried out since 1945 has not confirmed these claims, but this has not stopped the Spanish forest service from putting up some 300,000 boxes in Conservation Year.

Baron von Berlepsch also advocated making suitable nesting cavities in stone walls by means of cement 'nesting stones'. These would escape the effect of sudden changes in temperature which might chill broods in wooden boxes. My father's friend Jannion Steele Elliott may have got the idea from the baron. An authority both on birds and on restoring old houses, his trademarks were unobtrusive holes in the masonry,

still to be seen in walls by his Tudor house on the edge
of Wyre Forest.

Although it is tempting to laugh at the dogmatic
baron and his assiduous scribe, he set a fashion that
spread throughout northern Europe and had its counter-
part in North America.   It was soon discovered that
there was no special virtue in the woodpecker design,
and that tits and other hole-
nesters would accept almost
any box with a small
entrance and sufficient space
below it in which to build a
nest, if properly sited.
Elaborate 'rustic' accretions
were added externally to
please the eye of the human
beholder; in the form of
knobs or perches which
squirrels or stoats could grip
they were positively harmful.

By 1914 the nestbox had
become an accepted symbol
of bird protection, like the

Berlepsch open-fronted nestbox

hanging feeder and the bird table: metamorphosis
from the clay flask of Bruegel's time was complete.
But in the following year S. P. Baldwin and W. W.
Bowen began their study of the American house wren—
rather larger than our bird and a regular cavity
nester—and the nestbox found a third and most
important scientific role.   Hitherto the breeding of
such birds had been very difficult to record without
damage to the sites.   Boxes fitted with detachable lids
could be examined regularly; even more usefully,
their occupants, both adults and young, could be
caught, weighed, measured and ringed.   When the
Americans published their results a few years later they

had followed the lives of 180 individual wrens and had fitted recording devices to boxes to check the number of visits to the nest. In 1920, at Wageningen in Holland, K. Wolda began a long-term research project on the great tit, of which a whole local population will take to nestboxes. Carried on for many years by Dr H. N. Kluijver, the study is still going strong. At Oxford the Edward Grey Institute has been monitoring great and blue tits in Wytham Woods since 1948. The data for no two years are alike and the longer such projects last, the more is learned about the way in which populations fluctuate.

Tits are residents and inclined to be temperamental. The pied flycatcher is a summer visitor and ideal guinea-pig, submitting to constant examination and even the removal of part of its home for photography. When Lars von Haartman began 'boxing' them round his home in Finland in 1941, he started something which has led to the ringing of hundreds of thousands of flycatchers across Europe from Wales to Russia, where

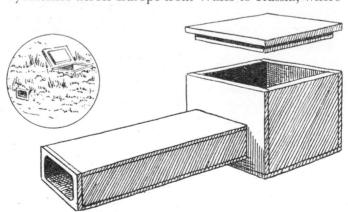

Tunnel nesting and observation box described in Edwin Cohen's field guide on 'Nestboxes' (British Trust for Ornithology, Beech Grove, Tring, Herts, 4s od)

these compliant birds have been experimentally transported. Numbers of young, some accompanied by adults, were moved by road or air in large cages to areas where pied flycatchers were previously unknown but which had suitable woodland. After a few days' confinement the birds were released, and some at least returned in succeeding years to occupy boxes put up in their new home. Pied flycatchers have also been watched at the nest by means of glass-backed boxes fitted to hides, and in both Russia and England have been induced to feed dummy nestlings.

The most complete study of a large bird by means of nestboxes is that of H. N. Southern, who wrote about it some years ago in 'The Countryman'. Using a chimney type slung under a sloping bough, he persuaded many of the tawny owl pairs in Wytham Woods to become his subjects. In Holland the use of large nestboxes on poles brought a much-needed population of kestrels and long-eared owls to combat a plague of voles on the new polders of East Flevoland. Some seventy pairs of kestrels have now nested—a fact which would have delighted Baron von Berlepsch, even though the boxes were not to his design. Large boxes mounted on poles in ponds and lakes have also been the means of repopulating much of eastern North America with the wood duck, and may yet assist the spread of the introduced mandarin in England.

The nestbox, whether as an aid to conservation or a tool for research, is a phenomenon of the northern hemisphere. Some ten years ago W. Buttiker tried to find out what success had attended nestboxes in southern Africa. The conventional types had attracted only isolated records of a few species, but hornbills, wood hoopoes, barbets and glossy starlings had occupied poles of the sisal aloe, *Agave sisalama*, fixed vertically to tree trunks about ten feet up. In New Zealand the introduced starlings and house sparrows will take over tit boxes, but the N.Z. robin has nested in the open-fronted type. There are reports of nestboxes put up in Indian forests, but I know no account of their effect.

Chimney-type nestbox

When Edwin Cohen and I wrote the first edition of the British Trust for Ornithology's field guide on nestboxes, we distinguished three main types. The enclosed space box, in different sizes, will attract about twenty-five British breeding birds; an extreme modification of it enabled David Lack to make his study of the swift in the tower of the Oxford University Museum. The open-fronted box is similar to that pioneered by Baron von Berlepsch. The chimney type, already mentioned, unfortunately attracts grey squirrels. More recently tunnel-type boxes have been tried out successfully for sand martins, wheatears and petrels. I am sure there are further modifications and gadgets to come. Wood remains the favourite material, though plastics, tin, asbestos sheeting and cement all have their advocates. Even in these days there are still 'firsts' to be achieved. As far as I know, the lesser spotted woodpecker has yet to nest in a British box, as has the hoopoe. A pair appeared near my house some years ago, and I put up two special boxes, but my only guests were starlings.

WILTSHIRE woman in bus stuck in traffic jam: ' 'Tis terrible in summer; you've got to get a bus too soon to get anywhere'.

Wild Life, Not Tame
by Stephen Dalton, F.R.P.S., A.I.I.P.

THE selection of wild life pictures is made particularly difficult by the many factors which must be considered. When examining the entries for this year's photographic competition I was looking for scientific authenticity, originality, technical quality and good composition; and even the winning entries fell short in one or more respects.

A natural history photograph must be scientifically authentic. It should show the animal or bird behaving naturally in its environment; and even if the creature is taken under controlled conditions, the background should appear authentic. Unfortunately what looks natural to the layman may look painfully rigged to the naturalist. I was also hoping to find originality: an animal doing something not often seen, or caught in an unusual attitude. But this is always difficult to achieve.

The technical quality of the print is most important, as natural history photographs in particular should convey as much information as possible to the viewer. They should be critically sharp; the sharper the picture, the more information it contains. Of course, there are exceptions. Certain action shots may benefit pictorially by slight blurring of wings, which can add to the feeling of movement. The accuracy of information conveyed by tonal separation is also important. Although the quality of the print depends largely on that of the negative, it is at the printing stage that most people go wrong. Distorted tones due to incorrect choice of paper grade are a common fault. A good print should contain a wide range of tones from solid black in the very deep shadows to pure white in the true highlights. Too much contrast results in large areas of 'blocked-up' blacks and toneless highlights with little gradation between the two extremes. Such pictures convey little information. On the other hand too soft a print has insufficient tonal separation, with dark grey shadows and light grey highlights, and gives a dull lifeless effect.

The final point I was looking for was good composition. The print should show that the photographer has a feeling for design. Also, wherever possible, the subject should stand out from its background; this is especially important if the print is to be reproduced. It presents one of the most difficult problems of wild life photography, because many creatures move about in places where they are naturally well camouflaged.

I was impressed by the wide variety of subjects tackled. They ranged from badgers peering out of sets to ladybirds feasting on greenfly. There were even photographs of tigers, bears and penguins, but these could hardly qualify as 'wild'. It was obvious that much trouble and time had been devoted to obtaining many of the photographs; for instance, there were several prints of badgers and foxes, and one of a golden eagle at its nest. Good photographs of such subjects require several days or even weeks of preparation, followed by patient waiting. But there were many pictures in which the animal or bird was far too large in the frame, with considerable areas of body either out of focus or out of the picture altogether.

I was sorry to find that a large number of potentially excellent photographs had been spoilt at the printing stage. Slightly fuzzy prints due to inaccurate focusing in enlargers, poor enlarger lenses or negatives not remaining flat during the printing exposure were too common. What grain structure there is should look sharp and gritty from the centre to the edge of the print. It is false economy to have a good camera and a second-rate enlarger or enlarger lens. Many photographs had been printed on the wrong grade of paper, or had large areas of dark or light tones which lacked detail and could have been greatly improved by shading or 'burning-in' during the printing. Some ninety-five per cent of negatives can benefit from such treatment. The composition of some of the prints could have been improved by further cropping under the enlarger.

When I had selected the eight entries reproduced on the following pages there was no obvious winner; all were good in their different ways. I awarded the prizes as follows:

First prize   A remarkable action shot of a blue tit in mid air, taken a split second before touch-down, after passing through the entrance hole of its nestbox. A purist might not consider a nestbox to be a strictly natural habitat; but the bird is 'wild, not tame', and so many blue tits now use nestboxes. Of all the entries this was the most original and unusual, and the print quality and definition of the photograph are excellent.

Second prize   Male orange-tip butterfly. Although static, this is a good example of a natural history photograph. The composition is excellent; the uncluttered background of out-of-focus varied tone makes the butterfly stand out well. Imaginative lighting shows up the texture of the wings. The definition and tonal quality of the print are outstanding—unsurpassed, in fact, by any other entry. It is unfortunate that some of this quality is bound to be lost in reproduction.

Third prize This picture of a fox cub is probably the most appealing of the three. The composition is good, and the subject stands out well against a background of light-toned grass. The print quality is excellent.

Anonymous

I CALL my cat Anonymous.
　He is the most discreetest puss,
The most secretive, neatest puss,
　And always has been so.

He never tells me where he goes,
Or what he knows, but leads and shows
His needs, then sits with tail-wrapped toes—
　Mi domine Ano!

But when he condescends to play
He's called Anon or Mousecadet
Or Anna-whom-three-realms-obey
　Or just Hey Nonny No.

He has his way; there is no fuss.
His name is not vouchsafed to us.
His age is just eleven plus
　And ever shall be so.

William Angus

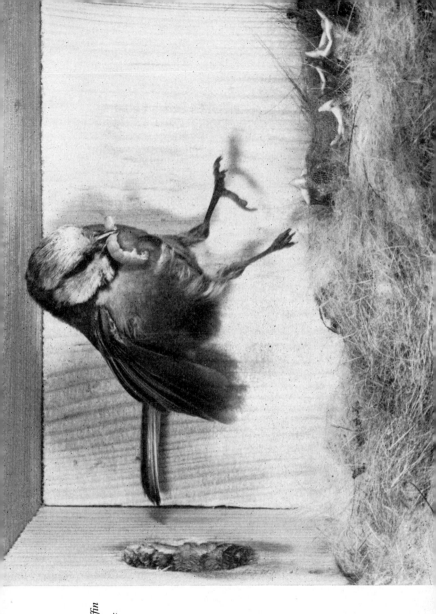

*FIRST
PRIZE*

**Blue tit
entering
nestbox**

James E. Tiffin

Goerz Tenax
Ilford FP4

SECOND PRIZE: orange-tip butterfly at rest on Bedfordshire hedgerow, by Richard Revels

THIRD PRIZE: fox cub at Silwood near Ascot, by Leonard J. Warner

GANNET ABOUT TO LAND ON BASS ROCK, FIRTH OF FORTH by Dennis Green

CRESTED TIT ON SPEYSIDE by Dennis A. Avon

Shield bug attacking sawfly larvae and (opposite) *lobster moth larvae, by Jane Craik*

FOX EMERGING FROM COPSE
by Leonard J. Warner

Calves on Approval
by A. V. Chadwick

THE farm was well off the beaten track in the
Ashdown Forest, and I was gazing at a singular
collection of young hybrid cattle which had been
assembled in a dilapidated outbuilding for my inspection.

'There y'are, then. Real pretty lot of 'eifers, ain't
they?'

Although this was a statement rather than a question,
it seemed to need some reply; and I had none. I
looked up at the lean leggy beasts in their rows of
small pens, deep in muck, and wondered how to tell
their sanguine owner, a lady of uncertain age, that
none of the animals would be eligible for the calf
subsidy.

My job as calf certifying officer took me all over
south-east England, and occasionally to areas as far
apart as Suffolk and Cornwall. I had to inspect
young cattle of certain breeds and crosses which were
submitted by farmers as being eligible for the subsidy.
The terms of reference were clear and specific, the
conditions excluding, *inter alia*, all pure dairy heifers;
only the use of the word 'reasonably' sometimes made
the judgement of dual-purpose animals a matter of
opinion rather than fact.

The present applicant, a black floppy straw hat
covering some of her lank straggling hair, waited in
growing dismay at my silence. When I slowly shook
my head she cried: 'What? Ef you don't pass they
'eifers I'll punch 'ee on the nose'.

I laughed and answered: 'Oh, I wouldn't do that.
I couldn't very well punch you back, could I? Look,
you put a bit of grub into them, and let me see them

L

again in a few months'. We parted on excellent terms.

It was quite typical of a day's work that I should go from a nobleman's estate with its large herd, modern buildings, manager and foreman, to old John Bloggs's small holding where I would find just two lovingly reared young steers of superb quality. But the moorland community around Bodmin, like their cattle, taxed my wits, adaptability and energy. The beasts presented to me were mostly Galloways of varying quality, shaggy and lively, which had been running wild without sight of man for the best part of the year. They were often not so much 'presented' as rounded up on horseback and rushed into some dark cobbled stable for me to wrestle with, before punching the required holes in their ears as best I could. Experience of the pain of being trampled by sharp hooves had taught me agility, but in Cornwall I had to learn that nervous young Galloways kick with both feet, like ponies. The secret of avoiding a nasty injury seemed to be to keep close to the little devils.

I also faced here a problem which was probably unique to Cornwall: the right ears of many beasts were already so perforated and cut about that some looked like oak leaves. When I demurred, suggesting that the subsidy must have been paid already on these animals, I was earnestly assured that the excisions were by way of owners' brand marks; many hundreds of cattle were running communally on the unfenced moorland.

The moor farmers were a close-knit inbred community. It soon came as no surprise when my first client of the morning not only spelt out for me my day's itinerary but filled in details of my route and brief character sketches of his neighbours—frequently relations—and the quality of the cattle I might expect to see. 'Then you'm goin' to Jan Pentreath—that's right, Trelawder Farm. Busy on 'is potatoes, 'e is. 'E wun't 'ave 'is cattle in ready for 'ee by 'leven o'clock, I c'n tell 'ee. Poor lot they be, tew.'

But the rough monotony of intractable black cattle was lightened by occasional visits to farms where neat red Devons or even rangy great South Devons predominated. Certainly it was the colour and variety of the farming pattern which prevented a strenuous job from ever becoming dull.

The Retreat of the Natives

SEVERAL holidays in Dorset had convinced my wife and me that, when our time came to retire, that was the county to settle in. Purposefully we visited it again last summer. The first hotel we tried was full, and the proprietor, a Canadian, referred us to people in the village. The lady of the house, from Sussex, could not accommodate us, so we went on to Bridport and found a nice room in an inn run by a Welshman.

The next morning, after sharing the breakfast room with a couple from Portsmouth and another from Cyprus, we called on an estate agent who hailed from Lancashire: he referred us to a builder from Coventry. We had lunch in a country inn kept by a couple from Sutton, who introduced us to the occupant (from Southampton) of the cottage opposite. Having refuelled at a garage with an Irish proprietor, we went to look at a house for sale: the occupant was born in Surrey.

It came as quite a shock, on visiting our farming friends in Symondsbury, to hear the genuine 'Darset' tongue.
—*Frank A. Lamb*

Hints for the Home Acre

This used to be among my prayers—a portion of land not so very large but which should contain a garden, and near the homestead a spring of ever flowing water, and a bit of forest to complete it—*Horace*. You plant and transplant and are dirty and amused—*Gray*

Variegated Leaves

IT may seem an odd time of year to mention Chelsea Flower Show, but I prefer to order new plants in the dormant season rather than when I see them exhibited. Then there is ample time to consider just how many you need to fill a gap, or if you can wait to grow them from seed. A day at any show can be exhausting and confusing unless you go through the turnstile with an aim in mind. This year I started with the intention of finding new ideas for the herbaceous borders and soon noticed that many of the plants which attracted my attention had variegated leaves. Now my gardening notebook contains a useful list of edging, as well as border, variegated plants, some more unusual and others old favourites. 'Edging' includes a few rock plants, as those can often be used to good effect in a border adjacent to the path, where you can enjoy them at close quarters.

Among the evergreens, so useful in winter, London pride (*Saxifraga umbrosa*) has variegated forms with leathery crenated leaves, mottled with yellow or cream. They thrive in sun and shade, but do not spread so rapidly as the common form, as most of the growth seems to be directed to making beautiful firm rosettes up to 9 in. across; ideally the plants should be treated as individuals rather than as carpeters. They are easily increased by removing the young shoots which develop close under each parent plant, and in this way each rosette is kept in perfect shape. *Erysimum linifolium* has a charming variegated form with yellow markings on the lance-shaped leaves. *Erysimum* is the Greek name used by Hippocrates, 'Father of Medicine', in 400 B.C.; but sometimes it is listed under *Cheiranthus*, the perennial wallflower, to which it is closely related.

Another pretty evergreen, *Veronica gentianoides variegata*, provides good ground cover for the front of the border, with glossy green leaves splashed with white and occasional pink, and delicate spikes of blue flowers in May and June. It is not quite so mat-forming as the plain-leaved variety, but cutting off the dead heads will help. It associates well with June-flowering shrubs such as the American beauty bush, *Kolkwitzia amabilis*, and pink deutzias, when planted in drifts round them.

To emphasise the line of a straight path nothing is easier or more effective than *Pulmonaria saccharata*. It is constant throughout the year and sends up its pink and blue flowers in early spring. I never realise just how many old flower stalks there are until I decide to remove them. This should be done; and immediately a crop of heart-shaped leaves, mottled all over with silvery cream, will appear. Several varieties are available with flowers in a range of colours; pretty as these are, it is the leaves which are all-important.

Two more evergreen plants which I find indispensable are *Vinca major elegantissima* and variegated ivy. The periwinkle can be allowed to ramp as ground cover, leaving every long stem to root where it touches down. It will soon make a yellow and green carpet, most effective round dark shrubs. We have it among a group of

Variegated ivy

hollies but, better still, I have seen it mingle with *Cotoneaster horizontalis*, its arching stems contrasting in shape and colour with the host's stiff herring-bone branches. If you do not want it to spread, it is quite easily restrained at the edge of a border, particularly at a stone or gravel path, provided you cut it back hard in spring. Then it will not wander, and it also seems to produce many more of its attractive blue flowers.

There are countless worth-while ivies, some with large leaves like *Hedera canariensis* Gloire de Marengo and *H. colchica dentata variegata*. Both need some help initially to climb, but once on their way they will look after themselves. They make a gorgeous splash of colour, especially welcome in winter. The first has silver-white markings, and the second yellow. A good way with the smaller-leaved ivies is to let them grow over a fair-sized stone at the front of the border where, before long, you will have an ivy cushion. I saw two particularly attractive varieties at Chelsea, both with well-marked and prettily shaped leaves, Golden Heart and *H. helix sagittaefolia variegata*.

Hosta undulata variegata

Among the herbaceous plants *Brunnera macrophylla* belongs to the same family as *Pulmonaria*, and at Chelsea I noticed the variety splashed with buff and light green. It is best used as a woodland plant, as the foliage becomes coarse and shabby by the autumn; but from April to July it has attractive forget-me-not-blue flowers. Solomon's seal, too, is best suited to a shady corner where it can have a cool root run, and there is a really elegant form with white-edged leaves. It would look lovely among my favourite hostas, *H. undulata variegata*, whose wavy leaves are generously marked with white. We tend to think of hostas as recent introductions, but this variety was brought from Japan as long ago as 1834; thirty years later it was illustrated in E. J. Lowe's book on 'Beautiful Leaved Plants'. But then, of course, they were called funkias.

There is an infinite variety of sedums; many are wonderful value, particularly the late autumn flowering kinds

S. kamtschaticum variegatum

which do not have an untidy moment until it is time to cut them down. *S. telephium variegatum* has glaucous green and buff leaves and 18-in. pink flowers in autumn. The exciting *S. sieboldii* is not reliably hardy, but *S. kamtschaticum variegatum* survives happily in the Cotswolds. This gay little plant has light-green leaves broadly margined with gold and a hint of orange, or perhaps it is only the reflection of the small orange buds which open star-shaped and yellow.—
Rosemary Verey

Salads out of Season

THERE is no reason why salads on side plates should not grace our meals even with the hottest dishes on the coldest days, as on the Continent. Once we stop thinking that salads mean only lettuce with cold mutton on Mondays, it is easy enough for any gardener to grow them round the year. If you have a cold greenhouse suitable for tomatoes in summer, you can begin by sowing the new Dutch lettuce Kwiek in the open early in August; transplant it between the tomato rows in September for cutting in November, January and February. Sow a couple of rows of Kloek in the greenhouse in October, prick out and eat until April. Leave space for a February sowing of Sutton's Windermere, the nicest of the frilly lettuces, to transplant when March starts going like a lamb, and begin the season again.

The basis of winter salads from the open garden is cabbage: not the January King and savoy hearts that fill the swill bins at nutritionally conscious schools, but the Monarchs which are bred for flavour raw as well as cooked. Although they cost about five times as much as ordinary varieties, you can sow the fewer seeds in a packet more thinly for better plants from uncrowded rows.

Sow Autumn Monarch in early May for October and November, and Winter Monarch at the end of May for December, January and February. Plant out 18 in. apart each way in staggered rows in July. If you have to wait for early peas or potatoes to release the ground, the seedlings can be set 6 in. apart in a waiting bed and moved with plenty of soil for a firm and final planting.

Next in flavour and hardiness are the red cabbages, with salad and vitamin values that are wasted by pickling. Red Drumhead and Stockley's Giant are both excellent for sowing and transplanting at the same time and spacing as Winter Monarch. Shredded with a sharp knife, they make an attractive contrast in a winter salad with mayonnaise, their delicate sweet flavour making them superior to rather tasteless forced greenhouse lettuce. They lead too on Vitamin C, with 60 mg. per 100 gm. against 18 mg. for lettuce; but this drops to 40 mg. after ten minutes' cooking, and to 15 mg. with the kind of boiling cabbages suffer in most cafés and hospitals.

Sprouting broccoli is even richer with 100 mg. raw in salad, but only 22 mg. after cooking. Sow Early Purple or White in late May and transplant in August, at 2 ft intervals in rows 30 in. apart, for picking from February until they run to yellow flowers as April ends. Give each plant a stout stake, like a dahlia, in windy gardens and pick only the flower heads with about two thirds of their stems, leaving the leaves to feed more shoots and to protect them from hard weather. This kind of broccoli has some resistance to clubroot—an advantage in many gardens.

Lettuce has much more Vitamin A than cabbage, with 540 against only 150 International Units per 100 gm., but broccoli scores 7000 and kale up to 20,000 I.U. Only one kale is nice enough to be eaten raw—the rare Russian Kale with lacy leaves entirely unlike the curled Scotch type and leafy bunches of shoots, for picking like sprouting broccoli, among the main leaves. Sown and grown just like the broccoli, it is ready from January onwards.

With the leafy basis in the bowl, grated raw roots can add further flavour and colour. Use a modern square-type stainless-steel grater, which is simplest to clean, and prepare immediately before serving. Sow a good keeping carrot like James Intermediate in June and, after October lifting, store in dry peat, which is far better than ashes, sand or sawdust.

I make no apology for mentioning again that finest root salad Cook's Delight beet, so called because it is best uncooked and never bleeds; a large one can remain in the fridge for a fortnight of grating without loss of its sweeter flavour and its betain, which replaces choline, a vitamin found in the organ meats that vegetarians miss. Sow in early June, 1 ft between rows and sparsely, for they should be thinned to 6-8 in. At this time and spacing sow a garden swede, such as Purple Top, for golden-yellow colour and a flavour which is nicer raw than cooked. Both roots are best sown to follow other crops in summer, so that they have time to grow without becoming woody monsters.

Not only diabetics and slimmers gain from daily salads in winter. What we eat raw holds catalase, the protective factor against cancer that is destroyed by cooking, and all the Vitamin C, which modern popular diets can lack in winter.—*Lawrence D. Hills*

Growing Camellias

I HAD always wanted to grow camellias but, like so many people, thought that they were delicate conservatory plants. Not until I came to live in South London and saw a large healthy camellia bush in my neighbour's garden, did I realise that they are one of the hardiest, yet most attractive, of all shrubs. They will grow almost anywhere, except in a chalky or lime-predominant soil, and are quite happy in built-up areas. A restricted root run suits them, so they do well in containers, provided that they are given plenty of soft water and the correct nutrients; but stone containers should not be used.

My camellias grow under trees—planes, lilac and cherry—where they get afternoon sun and the light freckled shade they like; the blossoms are easily damaged by wet or by frost melted in the morning sun. The soil is loamy, well-drained, inclined to dryness, so summer watering and mulching are essential. Plenty of peat was dug in before planting, and a mulch of leaf mould and grass cuttings given in summer. The grass should not be applied until well rotted and dried out. The whole bed has been underplanted with *Anemone blanda*, the small wild cyclamen and hostas of various kinds, all of which look delightful beneath the glossy camellia plants.

Many experts do not believe in feeding camellias, other than by dressing with compost, well-rotted stable manure or leaf mould; and mould which includes oak leaves is particularly good. The use of artificial fertilisers can be dangerous, and bonemeal is unsuitable, being too acid. Specially mixed and balanced fertilisers can be bought from firms specialising in camellias, and are best applied in spring or early summer.

There are hundreds of varieties from which to choose, many of them dating back to the late eighteenth century when camellias were first introduced to England. These include such excellent kinds as *C. japonica imbricata* (red, very double and formal, medium upright growth), *fimbriata* (white, with frilled petals, slow growing and bushy) and Lady Hume's Blush (blush pink, formal, small flowers, loose growth).

The great era of the camellia was in early and mid Victorian days, when the plants were usually grown in greenhouses and conservatories, although in one of my early gardening books, 'The Greenhouse' by Charles McIntosh (1838), it is stated that 'they will flower and grow well in the open air . . . and the day may not be far distant when the camellias will be found as much the ornament of our shrubberies as the *Pyrus japonica* and *Aucuba japonica*'. Victorian favourites still in the catalogues are *donckelarii* (red with white blotch, semi-double flower, medium growth), *alba plena* (lemon-white, formal double flower, bushy growth), Imperatrice Eugenie (pink-edged

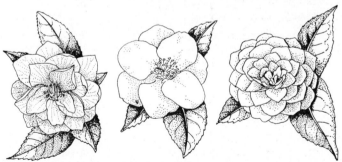

Camellias: (l. to r.) semi-double, single and formal double

white, anemone-flowered, spreading growth), Marguerite Gouillon (pale pink striped with carmine, peony flowered, like the old-fashioned *Rosa mundi*) and *elegans* (pink with a white marbled spot, neat growth). More than 250 varieties are listed in 'The Greenhouse', many of them still in cultivation.

Now there are a host of new names, and many come from the U.S.A., where camellias are extremely popular and numerous fine new varieties have been bred, usually with transatlantic names such as High Hat and Spanked Baby. Hybrids, especially the *williamsii* kinds, are particularly beautiful, some of the most attractive being Donation (clear rose pink, large semi-double flower, vigorous upright growth, small leaf), J. C. Williams (single pink flower, upright growth) and Inspiration (pink, semi-double, medium size), while the *sasanqua* group, mostly early blooming, can be particularly lovely, with their small leaves and single or semi-double flowers.

Propagating camellias can be tricky, since they need much humidity if cuttings are to succeed, and so far I have not managed to root cuttings; but I have two well-grown seedlings, which have not yet flowered. Even if they take time, camellias in leaf are handsome enough, and my two youngsters look so healthy and sturdy that I am content to wait and hope. They can take five or more years to bloom.

I find no plant more rewarding to the eye all the year round than the camellia, with glossy evergreen leaves through the winter, exquisite flowers in late winter or spring—I have had *alba plena* in flower when snow was on the ground—followed by brilliantly green young leaves in summer; and by autumn the next year's flower buds, fat with promise, sit like green chrysalids in the axils of their shining leaves. For me they have all the old-world charm and interest of the shrub roses—a personality, but also a more exotic splendour.—*Margaret Stanley-Wrench*

Airway to Aran
by Daphne Pochin Mould

OF all my approaches to little islands, this was the easiest. An island to me is a challenge. I have jumped from small boats on to wet cliff ledges in the Hebrides, I have been soaked by spray in home-built Irish currachs, felt the wind icy over Faroese tide-races and seen the sun smite on the wine-dark Aegean. 'Uniform Echo, clear to go', said the air traffic controller, and I took the little plane off from the vast expanse of Shannon's jet runway. Thirty-five minutes later her wheels were bumping over hard sand on one of the Aran islands in the mouth of Galway Bay—the latest group of islets to move into the air age.

If you think about it, the whole relationship between man and islands is one of communications. So many of the wild rocky islets round Irish and British coasts have a wealth of ruins; and not all have arrived at this state owing to some climatic change, some coast erosion. For primitive men the islands were good places to live; their light soils were easy to till, and the sea was a natural defence as well as a source of food. It was often easier to travel by water than in the woods and bogs of the mainland. Today even the most attractive island is likely to be abandoned when the standard of living falls markedly below that on the adjacent mainland, and too few people remain for the community to function properly. For Mykines in the Faroes the critical figure is the number of active men needed for the sheep round-up. It is expensive and sometimes difficult to get things, especially livestock, to market. 'We often accept a lower price than we should, rather than go to the expense of shipping the cattle home again from the

Limestone karst country, with coaster high above tide mark, on Inisheer

mainland market', said a farmer on one of the islands in the mouth of the Fergus river in Ireland.   Secondary school means boarding school; sickness or accident carries an element of crisis unknown to the main-lander.

The Blaskets were abandoned in the 1950s—the melancholy fade-out of a little community with a great tradition of island living and Irish speaking. Dursey island off the Cork coast may yet be saved by the cable-way lately constructed over the narrow sound through which the tides race; it will carry cattle as well as people, avoiding the losses, in both condition and life, involved in swimming the animals over.

The Aran islands, Irish-speaking, still building and sailing the currach, the canvas successor of the skin-covered canoe of ancient times, were not too badly off.   A regular big boat comes out from Galway, but only the largest island, Inishmore, has a pier to receive her; the other two must rely on transhipment by currach.   In recent years a helicopter has been available for serious accident calls anywhere in Ireland. Then in August the strip was ready, the sand levelled, and the grass and clover had become well established to bind it together. The nine-seater 'Islander' aircraft from Oranmore, on the mainland near Galway, began its regular daily commuting back and forth. There was a new route to the Isles.

On the first day of September, after a week of waiting, I got both the weather and the aircraft right and became the first woman pilot to land on the new airstrip. The three islands appeared ahead, dim shapes still, as we looked down on bogs bright with heather in flower and a blue sea breaking white on a strand. We saw the sheer drop of the cliffs of Moher, the far-off line of the Twelve Bens in Connemara and the islands coming close now. On Inisheer, the most easterly, a big coaster had been cast high above the tide mark by a freak storm, and its fittings can be seen in every house in the island.

Currachs and 'Morane', and 'Islander' partly obscured by fire-tender

Inishmaan, the middle island and the most isolated, is to have its airstrip next year.

On Inishmore, the big island, the sandy strands by Kilronan have a small headland between them; and across it lay the new strip with the 'Islander' parked alongside a red fire-tender. I circled, came in low and slow, cut the power, eased up the nose, and the 'Morane' settled on the grass, rolling a short way as I braked to a halt and turned her, to park beside the 'Islander'. This carries the new company's name in Irish letters, Aer Arann.

Just above us was an ancient stone chapel, dated back to *c.* 700 A.D., and on the edge of the great cliff line the famous stone fort of Dun Aengus. Other massive stone forts and, less obvious, old church sites of the Irish saints are dotted over the limestone karst uplands of the islands. Close to the site of the landing strip St Enda founded a great monastery about 500. A.D. It was one of the first monastic foundations in Ireland, seminal institutions which turned the country into a land of monasteries and monks. A whole litany of famous Irish saints is said to have come to study at them. Today little remains on the site—a fragment of a noble high cross and some ruined church walls; the 80-ft round tower fell in an island storm in the early nineteenth century. The legend makes it the starting point for the voyage of St Brendan the Navigator; and we can be certain that Brendan and his like did run their small boats ashore through the surf on these strands before they set off for adventurous landfalls.

I wanted to know what difference the fact that one could now fly easily into the islands would make to the people living there. More visitors, of course, will come in and out, but residents are experiencing a new ease of movement. Supplies of fresh food can be flown in. In winter, when the regular sailing

Stone fort among rocks, small houses and tiny fields on Inishmaan

is only twice weekly, an islander will no longer have to find a couple of nights' accommodation on the mainland; he can fly out in the morning, do his business and be home that evening. The plane will come cheaper than the special helicopter charters for emergencies. I thought of the people going to and from hospital, whose ailments would not justify the 'chopper' but for whom the air would provide a much easier and quicker road than the boat rolling in the rough waters of Galway Bay. 'I don't think it will fundamentally change the islanders' way of life': this was the verdict of one Aer Arann pilot. Some islanders are still a little suspicious—unsure—of the new road to and from the Isles; but the plane will become just as much a part of regular island transportation as the canvas currachs and the Galway boat.

I flew along the islands, past bare limestone rocks

which have a peculiar textural quality all their own, past the small houses and tiny fields. They form a hard background to living; of a total area of 18 sq. miles only six are cultivated, and peat for fuel has to be imported from Connemara. Tourism is important, and a quick air service in and out could make all the difference to those who want to live on the islands. I flew on, round the coast of Connemara and up Clew Bay. It was islands, islands, all the way—islands where people still live, deserted islands with ruined Celtic monasteries, ruined farms and the patterns of stone walls, places where the struggle of living had proved too much for the islanders. Next year I may land on Inishmaan.

Reservoir

THEY built at valley's end a wall to keep
  Captive the stream, and then the waters filled
Slowly the chequered floor and buried deep
Furrow and hedgerow, pasture land and tilled.
Season gave place to season passing by,
And grass and tree to fish and water-weed,
Until the surface mirrored cloud and sky,
Mature and beautiful, a lake indeed.

Now from a lakeside window I behold
Across a tended lawn the shining thing,
The hills its cradle, fold on grassy fold,
The woodlands turning emerald in spring,
And creatures of the mere in westward flight,
And red sails in a twilight dying to night.

Eric Chilman

Wild Life and Tame

Open the book of nature where you will, and at any period of your life, and if you have the desire to acquire knowledge you will find it of intense interest . . . in nature there is no finality—*Jim Corbett*

TUBBY REDIVIVUS. One morning I failed to notice that a goldfish was missing from the tank. Evidently it had jumped out during the night and flapped its way across the floor, for at about 11.30 I saw a mysterious bit of gold under the refrigerator. I pulled it out and was only just able to recognise Tubby, who was six years old and reared from spawn in the tank. Now he was flattened out and covered in fluff, lacking most of his scales, down to raw flesh on one side, eyes protruding, bearing all the signs of death and *rigor mortis*. On the way to bury him I stopped and gently squeezed the upper part of his stiff body in my hand. After working for just over 20 minutes, I thought I detected a faint flicker. At first I dismissed it as imagination; then it happened again. But as soon as I stopped my artificial respiration, Tubby 'died'; so I continued with the pumping, alternately just under water and on the surface. Gradually I could feel the fish's body loosening and beginning to fill out, until there was a slight movement of the gills and a tiny bubble was released. After ten more minutes he brought up some transparent mucous and immediately tried to use his fins, but he was unable to stay upright, rolling over and floating on top of the water when I removed my hand. I continued my support, slowly taking him down deeper. Next time I let him go, he remained upright but tended to float upwards, so I chased him round the tank, causing the release of a lot of bubbles. After a short rest I repeated the treatment, and it worked; Tubby began to swim almost normally, ate a tiny piece of raw meat and made rapid progress. But next morning his scaleless body seemed to have gone septic, and he was again lethargic. Lifting him out, I gently stroked the mould from his body in clean salt and water. He became quite lively, but I had to repeat the treatment daily for ten days. After three weeks he was fit enough to join the others in the mad mating-season chase, but he was not a goldfish any more; his new scales were silver. Traces of gold reappeared on fins, tail and head nine weeks after his accident.—*Joan Blewitt Cox, Devon*

*O*LLY AND OCK. One August we acquired a status symbol in the form of a little owl, probably a juvenile, who would sit for half an hour on a little stone wall not 20 yds from our open window. Visitors stopped sipping tea to cry, 'Look, there's an owl!' and we would nonchalantly reply, 'Oh yes, that's Olly'. Sometimes he would drift down to the lawn to pick up an insect or run along, rather like a penguin, to snatch one in motion. His appearances were greeted by a commotion from the other birds, and strangers would dive-bomb him, causing him to hunch into his shoulders if they came too close. When the mobbing became too hot, he would quietly sweep off to a partly hollow ash about 100 yds away. This became the nest-site next spring when, after a winter's absence, Olly returned with a lighter-coloured mate, Ock. One after the other my cherished garden nests surrendered: first the blue tits in the copper beech when Olly took to perching on their nest-box; finally the sparrows under the guttering. I was woken very early by a terrific noise to find Olly sitting alongside the nest only a few feet from me. He made for the old ash with a *que-e-ek* of alarm. Here the owls were now busy in the dusk feeding their brood, hunting for insects among the roses and other flowers. One evening in mid July my resentment of the predatory pair vanished, when I saw on the dead branch usually occupied by Olly and Ock three fluffy little bundles, looking rather like See, Speak and Hear No Evil; one parent sat below and one above them. Soon they were perching on the hay bales, one here, one there, to be fed in turn, until the day when they all disappeared. We continued to hear them hunting on mild nights through the autumn and winter.— *Betty Cohen, Glamorgan*

*D*UCKS IN THE BATH. After a night with 22° of frost two white-faced tree ducks were covered with ice and wearing skirts of large icicles. I picked them up— like all my forty-two kinds of wildfowl, they are very tame— and put them in our bathroom. They were unalarmed by their surroundings and excited by the very warm bath I gave them. Having thawed out, they tried to hop up on the side of the bath, found it too slippery and fell on the floor. A bath towel hanging over the edge cured this, and the ducks approved with penetrating whistles. I put food on the floor, and the take-over was complete. Next day a partly frozen duck Chiloe wigeon joined the tree ducks and was soon a new bird. She was followed by a duck cinnamon teal who had been repeatedly covered with ice, but

Ducks in the bath: (l. to r.) cinnamon teal, Chiloe wigeon and tree duck

soon recovered. I was sorry for her mate; unlike the
Chiloe drake, who had taken the opportunity of his duck's
absence to break up another mated couple, the teal was a
faithful spouse. So after a day or two I brought him into
the bathroom. His mate, who had been eating on the
floor, waddled towards him; he advanced slowly and they
met with teal-like noises, knocking beaks in affection. The
duck then hopped on a log, placed there as an approach,
and called the drake to follow. He joined her and a little
'chat' took place. Next she popped on to the edge of the
bath, he followed, and both went down into the water.
The changing of the water every other day apparently
provided great excitement for the ducks. They usually
perched round the edge, watched the water run out and
listened to the gurglings. As the fresh water ran in, the
tree ducks whistled loudly, the wigeon stood first on one
foot and then on the other, and the teal grunted to each
other. When the bath was full and the tap off, they all
dropped in, splashing wildly, preening and flapping their
wings. Finally a complete tidy-up took place on the edge
of the bath.—*Rosemary Upton, Essex*

*B*ITTERN ON ICE. One
cold but sunny day last
winter a bittern suddenly
walked out of the reeds at the
Leighton Moss reserve of the
Royal Society for the Protection of Birds. I expected it to
dodge back almost at once, but
it started to feed by pecking at
something—presumably insects
which had hatched in the
sunshine—on the stems of the
reeds. The freezing of the mere
provided the bird with a
platform a foot or so above its
normal standing level, and
parts of the reeds normally
beyond its reach were now
accessible. Stimulated by these
conditions, the bittern hurried
to and fro, pecking busily,
then jumping to reach high up
the reeds and positively rushing
across the ice. Several times it
slipped and had difficulty in
recovering its balance; then,
after a particularly energetic
dash, it sat down with a bump
and went sliding across the ice on
its back, its big feet waving in
the air in a quite ludicrous
manner. Twice more this
happened before the bittern
apparently decided that it was

out of its element and returned to the shelter of the reeds.—*Tom Atkinson, Lancashire*

SHORT HAZARD. While walking in the south of France, dressed in shorts, I felt a tickling sensation on the front of my leg. Looking down, I saw a grey bush-cricket, about 1½ in. long, perched on the top of my sock and apparently busy feeding off my leg. There was no sensation of being bitten, just tickled, and on closer examination I could see the insect's jaws working sideways in a scuffing action. Whether it was getting any skin or merely scooping up salty sweat, I could not decide; there was no visible mark on my leg afterwards. Normally these insects are shy and jump away from an approaching hand, but this one would not move even when pushed, and had to be forcibly removed.—*J. Dingle, Yorkshire.* [This is a most unusual observation. The bush-cricket was probably licking up moisture with its maxillae.—*John Burton*]

PLAYING BALL. Off North Ronaldsay to the north of Orkney lies a skerry, home of a colony of grey seals. While I was watching them one day, a crofter-fisherman friend told me that they did a great deal of damage to lobster pots. When leaping and playing, they became entangled with the ropes, twisting and shortening them so much that the floats were held under at high water and could not be located. I felt this was rather a tall story until, some months later, I was on Glimpsholm at the eastern end of Scapa Flow. Bobbing on the pale blue winter sea was a large fluorescent orange float, marking a lobster pot and making a brilliant splash of colour in the sunshine. The head of a large seal appeared near the float and the animal proceeded to cruise round it, dive close to it and push it with its nose, twisting this way and that and finally disappearing, as did the float. I watched for some time, and again on my way home, but the float did not reappear.—*M. Traill-Clouston, Orkney*

BEATING THE FREEZE. In a very cold spell one winter the moorhens moved up from the burnside to feed at bird tables in our garden. Four could cause a traffic jam so, to relieve pressure, I scattered maize meal, bird seed and brown breadcrumbs on the lawn for them. The cold grew intense, but around midday the sun melted the thin crust of snow a little, and there was a film of moisture on the ice. An hour or so later all was hard again, and only sparrows and finches could detach particles of food from the frozen ground. The moorhens, who had previously eaten on the move, now 'brooded' for several minutes at a time, rising and eating from where they had crouched, before walking a few paces and brooding again. This pattern of feeding continued while the severe conditions lasted. Surely they were using their own body heat to thaw out their meals?—*Sydney R. Davidson, Perthshire*. [Moorhens appear to be intelligent as well as highly successful birds. A recent note in 'British Birds' described how an incubating moorhen picked up and shielded its back with a piece of plastic material whenever it rained.—*B. C.*]

DEFROSTED. Among the birds feeding in the garden during a snowy spell was a female pied wagtail encumbered by a ball of ice on one foot, which seemed to stick to the ground when she stood still for a few minutes. I put out some fresh water and, after a preliminary examination, she stepped in without bothering to drink. After several paddles her foot was free but, instead of going away, she ate some crumbs and returned to the water for more paddles; though it was not much above freezing, it may have seemed warm to her.—*Winifred Dixon, Norfolk*

TO AND FRO. We were sitting in the car outside Swyncombe Church, near Ewelme in Oxfordshire, at 12.30 one day in August when a weasel ran out of the churchyard and across the road, carrying what appeared to be a full-grown long-tailed field mouse. It returned at 12.35 without the mouse, and at 12.45 dashed over with a second. During the next 56 minutes it brought out five more mice and what looked like a young rat about 4 in. long excluding the tail. Sometimes it took only three minutes to make a capture, but its final visit to the churchyard occupied nearly 18 minutes and it emerged at 1.41 without prey. We waited another 50 minutes, but did not see the weasel again.—*Douglas Carr, Surrey*

TWO-FOOT STANCE. One February afternoon a group of starlings were trying to feed on a long and tough meat scrap on my lawn. One would peck at the meat without securing it; another would hold it with a foot and attempt to eat. As a result the scrap was tossed about, no bird actually swallowing any of it. Then a newly arrived starling stood with a foot on each end of the scrap and, by pecking between them, managed to eat a good proportion before other aggressive birds pulled it away, to be tugged about the lawn again. Later the successful bird got the meat back and at once stood on both ends; held like this, the meal was quickly finished.—*Philip Radford, Bristol*

ON EARLSWOOD COMMON, SURREY
by Tony Boxall

HEDGING AT YSTRADFELLTE, BRECONSHIRE
by George H. Hall

DRIVING FENCING STAKE ON A COLD DAY
by Robert Miller

THORNTON FORCE (70 FT DROP) FROZEN SOLID
by Tom Parker

TRACKS IN THE SNOW
by Robert Miller

THE BEST BEDSPREAD by J. R. Barton

SIGNS OF SPRING AT CROOK O' LUNE, LANCASHIRE
by Vernon D. Shaw

The Oldest Living Things
by Bernard N. Bowden

THE redwood, affectionately known as the big tree, has symbolised their country to generations of Americans. These gigantic trees grow to more than three hundred feet and reflect the vast blue distances of the great plains and the scale of mountains and lakes of the Rockies. They live to more than three thousand years. Until the 1950s it was thought that this made them easily the longest-lived species on earth. It now seems that the African baobab and the American bristle cone pine have even longer life-spans.

The baobab, the tree Allah planted upside down, cannot rival the American redwoods in height. The largest David Livingstone saw was a mere sixty feet tall and eighty in girth. But the baobab is a very large tree by everyday standards; a hollow specimen in Rhodesia is used as a bus shelter and can accommodate up to forty people.

It was named *Adansonia digitata* after the botanist Adanson, who estimated the oldest to be the colossal age of five thousand years. Little reliance could be placed on this figure as he obtained it by counting growth rings, and it was not certain that those of the baobab were annual rings. In the dry tropics, where rainfall is irregular, it was conceivable that several might be formed in one year, perhaps even a different number for each year and place depending on the climate. So Adanson's age of five thousand years could be regarded only as possible but not proven. In 1963, however, E. R. Swart showed that he was probably correct: that the growth rings of the baobab are true annual rings due to the alternation of more rapid growth in the rainy season and slow growth in

M

the dry season. These conclusions were reached by the modern technique of radiocarbon dating, which has been used extensively for archaeological finds.

Briefly, the cosmic rays coming from outer space collide with atoms of nitrogen in the earth's atmosphere and transform them into atoms of carbon. This carbon derived from nitrogen is termed carbon fourteen or radiocarbon. It behaves in every respect like the normal carbon except that its atoms weigh fourteen units instead of the normal twelve, and that in the course of time it disintegrates. The proportion of carbon fourteen to carbon twelve in the atmosphere is minute but constant, because carbon fourteen is disintegrating as fast as it is formed. Plants build carbon into their tissues, so the newly produced plant tissues contain the same proportion of carbon fourteen as the atmosphere. The proportion does not stay constant in plant tissues, however, as the carbon fourteen continues to disintegrate and no more is formed in them. The proportion of carbon fourteen in a plant tissue such as baobab wood thus slowly and continuously decreases—so slowly, in fact, that it takes five thousand years for the proportion of carbon fourteen to fall to half of its original value. Since the rate at which carbon fourteen is lost from plant tissue is known, it is necessary only to measure the proportion of carbon fourteen in an old piece of tissue to be able to estimate its age.

Wood from the centre of a baobab fifteen feet in diameter which was cut down in the Kariba Dam project was found by radiocarbon dating to be about one thousand years old. Dating other samples of wood from nearer the periphery of the trunk showed that the growth rings were in fact annual rings, and that the largest baobabs must be several thousands of years old.

At about the same time tree scientists became interested in the ages of bristle cone pines, *Pinus aristata*, in the White Mountains of Nevada. Edmund Schulman of the University of Arizona in 1963 extracted cores of wood containing sections through the annual rings from the bark right to the centres of the trees. From annual ring counts made on these borings it was estimated that many trees were four thousand years old.

The taking of borings is not at all easy, as with a large tree it is difficult to be certain that the core passes through the centre, and the long holes tend to cause the borers to snap. To clinch matters the U.S. Forestry Service gave permission for a large bristle cone to be felled at Wheeler Park, Nevada, so that its annual rings could be accurately counted and dated. There were 4900 of them so that, on the fairly safe assumption that not more than one ring was produced each year, this tree must have been at least 4900 years old at the time of felling.

Last year V. C. La Marche showed that these very old bristle cones are confined to the tops of mountains, where the soil is shallow and rocky and as a consequence very dry. Lower down, where the soils are deeper, moister and more fertile, there are bristle cones, but only comparative youngsters. For this reason these high dry mountain tops have been called the 'old-age habitats'. As they lie at about ten thousand feet above sea level, there is a great deal of wind, which tends to kill off branches and to abrade the trunks with dust and ice particles on their down-slope sides. After about fourteen centuries these trees seem to give up the attempt to add wood all round their trunks and grow only on the sheltered up-slope sides. The trunks thus become more and more plank shaped.

At low altitudes the down-slope deadwood succumbs

relatively early in life to wood-rotting fungi because of the moister warmer conditions; but the harder denser wood produced by slower growth is more resistant to fungal decay, especially in the cold dry conditions of the mountain tops, so that the dead wood continues to support the living part of the trunk much longer. Also the slower growth at these high altitudes leads to the formation of shorter branches and smaller crowns, so fire does not jump from tree to tree so readily as in the more luxuriant forests of the lower slopes.

There are many similarities between the life conditions of baobabs and bristle cones. The first also occupy a dry habitat with a moderate rainfall concentrated into a few months of the year; at other times there is no rainfall at all. So a short growing season causes relatively slow growth. The aridity causes competition for water between baobabs, which therefore tend to be widely spaced. This, together with their thick bark, also prevents them from being destroyed by fire. On the other hand fungal decay of the dead wood does not seem to be slowed to any significant extent, as most old baobabs are hollow shells.

The recipe for the long life of these two species seems to be a slow rate of growth, together with an absence of lethal factors such as fire, which would kill them before they had attained their potential life-spans.

SNAP JUDGMENT. From report of parish council meeting in Hampshire paper: 'In reply to questions about the public rights of way, the speaker assured the audience that it is illegal to keep a bull more than a year old in a field that has a right of way through it. She suggested examining its teeth when trying to assess the animal's age'.

Night Walk

R AGS of cloud
   polish the moon bright;
trees whimper, cowed
like dogs chained out at night;
the grass rustles a warning
and is still;
an owl hoots, mourning
the passing of its kill.

The woods watch me as I pass,
seeming to hold their breath;
the silence in the grass
listens to my footsteps and death
pauses. The hunted pant in flight;
behind me a sigh, a shriek;
the beat of wings on the night
brushing past seek
and prey in the wind and the rain;
the whimper rises to a howl;
raindrops crackle on the lane;
and again I hear the owl.

I wade through the dark
to where the waves
of rolling hills mark
distant architraves
of clouds and trees;
and high beyond a glow
that reddens the air and sees
the village far below.

T. J. C. Dennis

Snake in the Glass
by Joan Kent

MY brother warned me of the snake inside our lamp. At night it was clearly visible coiled up in the translucent bowl and, when the lamp was filled, I could see it squirming like the viper we once found behind the water-butt.

The lamp had a base of twining iron vines and a multi-coloured globe that radiated light like sunshine through stained glass. It transformed our workaday farmhouse kitchen and was the axis of my childhood's winter world. I treated it with healthy respect, knowing that the snake waited like some evil genie in a bottle, ready to escape and eat whoever broke the lamp. The memory of that Saturday night when it was smashed is with me still.

My mother believed that, if her children started each Sunday clean inside and out, nothing would ail them for the rest of the week. Each Saturday after tea the galvanised tin bath was placed on the flag-stoned scullery floor between the copper and the pump; and no matter how warm the water, one had the sensation of sitting on a cold wet slab. Being the youngest, I came first in the assembly line, but all six of us eventually progressed to sit in cotton nightshirts, drying our hair in front of the kitchen fire.

Medicines for both humans and animals were lumped together on the same high shelf and, after baths were over, Mum lifted down a square yellow tin. This, according to its deceptive label, contained a brand of wonder lozenge that cured coughs, croup and consumption. Gathering us round her like a hen with worms for her chicks, Mum stood over us, ladling

out great lumps of green gritty liquorice powder into
cups of senna tea. We would have preferred the
worms. To our young minds Saturday night without
liquorice was the main attraction in marriage.

Anyone with a skin blemish was treated to a dose
of brimstone in black treacle as a Saturday evening
second course. The horses were sometimes given the
same mixture and, as Mum used to say, 'Show me a
horse with pimples'. Chilblains and sprains were
vigorously treated with rubbing oil; the label on the
bottle showing both horse and groom proved con-
clusively to Mum that it was intended for man and
beast. Many an egg-bound hen was galvanised into
frantic productivity for fear of receiving a second dose
of Mum's Saturday brew; and if the worm tablets in
the orange tin kept our big-boned Kentish sheep from

Saturday night's assembly line

liver fluke, they did the same for us. A passing vet had
once pronounced my sister 'weakly', and thereafter
she was dosed with blood-mixture and a patent food
for feeble calves.

At dosing time Dad lit the hurricane lamp and
took himself off to the stables. As the youngest,
I had my liquorice first; so it seemed downright unjust
that on the night of the rebellion mine was the only
cup to be emptied. My usually submissive sister stood
with lips shut tight, her flushed face turning interesting
shades of mauve as she defied the hands that held her
nose, after she had declared that death was preferable
to liquorice. In the scrimmage the contents of the cup
were flung across the table. There was a crack like
breaking ice on a frozen pond, and paraffin seeped
across the red velvet table-cloth. With a speed that
belied her size, Mum snatched the smoking lamp and
ran from the kitchen to hurl it on to the wet cobbles in
the yard. Firelit shadows crept across the beams of
the ceiling, as we children waited in the sort of calm
that lies in the eye of a hurricane. The tempest
struck. Mum, with copper-stick in hand and retri-
bution in her heart, sent all six of us trembling to our
beds.

Justice had been satisfied, the candles taken down,
and we lay rattling the knobs on our old brass bed-
stead. My sister sobbed from injured pride and a
sore seat; I lay shivering with fear. Somewhere in our
house that awful reptile was probably slithering around
in search of her, because she had broken the lamp and
set it free.

A more terrifying thought sent me scuttling out
of bed, along the dark passage, down the back stairs
and into the kitchen, unfamiliar now in the dull light
of a hurricane lamp. Dad sat in the high-backed
windsor chair and, almost incoherent, I scrambled to

the safety of his knee. When words would come I warned him that, although my sister had caused the lamp to be broken, it was Mum who had smashed it. I knew that Dad would not want the snake to eat her, because she was his friend. Only that week I had seen him kiss her in the barn.

Strangely he had no fears. He said the biggest snake in Kent was only half the length of his shepherd's crook, so it would be no match for our cottage-loaf-shaped Mum and could even get a dose of liquorice for its pains. To prove his point he reasoned that the whale-boned armour-plated stays Mum always wore would deter a rhinoceros, much more a slithering little snake.

Mum emerged from the scullery, pink-cheeked, her cotton nightgown buttoned

In the barn

to the neck, carrying her stays. I implored her to wear them night and day. She promised that she would, then held me close to her comforting feather-bolster front.

When I crossed the yard in the morning, I passed the shattered lamp, its wick still coiled up, in a rainbow puddle. It was replaced by a brass affair which gave a flat uninteresting light. The kitchen lost its magic, and its menace, from that day. Medicines we had in plenty, but never again Mum's Saturday brew.

Looking at Nature

These observations are, I trust, true in the whole, though I do not pretend to show that they are perfectly void of mistake, or that a more nice observer might not make many additions, since subjects of this kind are inexhaustible—*Gilbert White*

Birdwatchers' Quadrennial. When the International Ornithological Congress last met in Holland, in 1930, it had a membership of about two hundred. September's gathering in the palatial Netherlands Congress Centre at The Hague attracted some 850 members from forty countries, although Asia and Australasia were poorly represented. The host country, Britain and the U.S.A. provided nearly four hundred between them, and almost all the proceedings were in English; at the opening ceremony the burgomaster quoted from Keats's 'Ode to a Nightingale'. Films have become an important element in recent congresses and the B.B.C. allowed us a preview of 'The Baobab'. Alan Root's masterpiece recalled the impression made by Heinz Sielmann's woodpecker film at Basle in 1954. But Franz Sauer's slides of ostriches in South West Africa were even more sensational. Unusually heavy rains in March and April of last year led to a flush of vegetation which so stimulated these huge birds that they bred four months earlier than usual and continued in a state of sexual activity culminating in a second peak just when the first eggs were hatching. Chicks and juveniles were abandoned, or ruthlessly attacked if they tried to join the adults, and many wandered off in leaderless flocks of up to seven hundred birds. Dr Sauer told me that he also filmed this extraordinary event; the result must surely find its way on to our screens in due course.

There were plenty of birds to be seen in three dimensions on the mid-week excursions which broke up the intensive round of papers and discussions. Some 250 avocets feeding on the mud against a background of ducks, spoonbills and grey lag geese vied with a tight-packed flock of 5000 oystercatchers as the highlight of my day, during which I 'scored' twenty-two kinds of wader, from curlews to little stints. But the areas we visited are overshadowed by what our hosts call collectively the delta works; their effect on the bird life of south-west Holland remains to be seen. Some critics believe that the Congress has become too large. The holding of the next in Australia for the first time will certainly remedy that, and it remains a unique forum where the amateurs and the growing number of professional ornithologists mingle and acknowledge their common interest.

Acceptable Aliens.   Several topics generate heat among naturalists; the introduction of new species is one of them. The 'antis' point to the disastrous results of deliberate or accidental arrivals of both plants and animals in virgin environments, especially islands, leading often to the transformation of the landscape and the extinction of unique endemic forms.   The 'pros' concede the thoughtlessness of past actions, but consider that, where a virtually new habitat has been created, as in our forests of exotic conifers, it could legitimately be enriched by introducing, for example, some of the European forest birds which seem unable to cross the sea gap on their own.   There is less argument about reintroductions.   Only an extremist can regret the return of the capercaillie to the Scottish Highlands in 1837; and now reindeer, once hunted by the viking jarls on the moors and mosses of Caithness, have been accepted on a semi-domesticated basis on the Cairn Gorm hills, and the attempt of the Royal Society for the Protection of Birds to bring back the white-tailed eagle has been generally approved.   When it comes to wolves and bears there is less enthusiasm, but many naturalists would welcome the return of the beaver and perhaps the wild boar to suitable nature reserves.

The Conservation Liaison Committee of the Society for the Promotion of Nature Reserves, in their second technical publication, 'Policy on Introductions to Nature Reserves' (Manor House, Alford, Lincs, 1s 6d), discuss the problem which faces the various landholding bodies represented on the committee and the more progressive local authorities as well. The most cogent reason for introductions or transplants is to save individual species whose habitats are about to disappear. This applies principally to plants in their own right and as essential food for insects, but the booklet points out that the St Kilda race of the house mouse might have 'qualified under this heading and that other island subspecies might well do so'. Other reasons for introductions are to prevent the erosion of sites like sand dunes, to create new habitats in the interests of ecological diversity, for experiments, and occasionally to provide a crop where part of the area is managed as farmland or economic forest. The booklet lays down criteria under

Capercaillies in the Scottish Highlands

these headings and recommends procedures which include documentation on the standard cards issued by the Nature Conservancy's Biological Records Centre. Accidental arrivals will inevitably continue in this imperfect world, but they can at least be recognised if the deliberate introductions are properly recorded.

Thoroughly at Home. Over much of the British Isles we have inherited a haphazard situation in which introductions of both native and foreign species have been carried out at the whim of landowners or as by-products of various kinds of development: the spread of Oxford ragwort along our railway system is the classical example. Sometimes an alien will succeed where nothing else can. Such woodlands as our remoter islands possess owe a great deal to what, as students in Edinburgh, we were taught to call the Scots maple, probably because it was introduced from continental Europe to Scotland—where most people call it the 'plane'—before England welcomed it under the equally inaccurate name of sycamore. By the middle of this century Miles Hadfield was able to write that it 'seems to be the only indisputably introduced tree that is perfectly naturalised over most of Britain and able not only to maintain itself but to increase'. Its successes include the most northerly grove of tree height in Shetland, at Halligarth on Unst, Orkney's most extensive woodland at Balfour Castle on Shapinsay, where it is mixed with ash, alder, rowan and even horse chestnut, and the woods round Bridgend on Islay, where wych elm is its associate. These man-made stands lack a shrub layer and have a field layer of ferns (other than bracken) and grasses, giving them a characteristic 'facies'. Sir Arthur Tansley had nothing to say about them in 'The British Islands and Their Vegetation', presumably because of their origins; yet to the ecologist they are a unique habitat and have been responsible for the spread of several woodland birds and, no doubt, of invertebrates as well. When Maury Meiklejohn and J. K. Stanford rediscovered the ornithological richness of Islay in 1954, it was in the Bridgend woods that they found three kinds of owl, nightjar, long-tailed tit and goldcrest, wood warbler and chiffchaff, and had reports of the great spotted woodpecker; to these the collared dove has now added its voice, as it has at Balfour Castle.

Where indigenous trees prosper the sycamore can become a nuisance, and it is Nature Conservancy policy to remove it on reserves like Roudsea Wood by the river Leven in North Lancashire, in which an astonishing variety of natives is the great attraction. The National Trust for Scotland might also take a look at the Pass of Killiecrankie where I was surprised recently to see the profusion of sycamore saplings. Here the Highland oak-birch association should be allowed to dominate. In the south of England the sycamore has become somewhat ironically the victim of another alien, the grey squirrel, and I know one woodland owner who is leaving it as a constituent in his mixed stands to divert the squirrels from ash and other natives.

The Island Bug. Sark was reputedly bare even of gorse when Helier de Carteret took over the island in 1567. A number of its narrow valleys are now so well wooded as to seem a different, secret world from that of the exposed plateau and bastion sea cliffs. Here too sycamore has played its part, with elm and ash, and ivy adds its sombre colour, creeping over the ground and up the trunks. These valleys are the haunt of the short-toed treecreeper, the only non-British land bird which the Channel Isles can

Chiffchaff on branch of sycamore

claim.   This is part of the fascination that the smaller
islands hold for naturalists: the possibility of some quirk of
distribution, or the evolution of a special race.   They also
have a sharply defined area which seems susceptible to a
thorough going-over in a comparatively short time.   The
flora of Sark was listed a few years ago for La Société
Guernesiaise by Frances Le Sueur and David McClintock,
and the butterflies as recently as 1966 by C. J. Shayler.   I
do not claim, on a week's visit in late summer, to have made
much impression on the plants, but did manage to see
twenty of the thirty-one butterflies on the list, which include
four or five rare visitors.   None that I saw was in that
class but the good season commented on last quarter,
together with an apparent absence of insecticides, seems to
have been responsible for the fine show of common kinds.
Not since schooldays had I seen the silver-studded blue,
which flies among the patches of bell heather on the cotil,
the rough ground between the plateau and the cliffs; and
the late brood of the pearl-bordered fritillary was another
pleasure.   All we saw of the island's lesser white-toothed
shrew, which it shares with Jersey and Scilly, was the lower
half of one lying on a path.   There was in the same spot a
mysterious bat, larger than the pipistrelle, which is the
common Sark species.   On a bare headland I found
droppings of what I presumed to be the black rat, now
almost extinct in Britain, and evidence of rabbits was

everywhere, though the animals themselves seemed to be remarkably nocturnal.

Sark was fortunate to capture Frank Rountree six years ago to become its resident naturalist. His particular interest is birds and, with the help of a small committee of observers, he has raised the island's species total from fewer than 100 to nearly 150, to which I was surprised and delighted to add one, the redshank. A full list is to be published shortly. On Islay we found Gordon Booth in much the same position, though with a larger province. His enthusiasm for the thousands of geese that winter on the island led him to migrate from Yorkshire. Now he finds himself organising the field work for the British Trust for Ornithology's atlas of breeding distribution, involving

Silver-studded blue

fourteen 10 km. squares. Even though several of them are mainly sea, they take some covering, for Islay, most fertile of the Hebrides, has nearly as many breeding birds as the whole of Ireland.—*Bruce Campbell*

Hold-up

THE stile had at last been mended and the stream bridged, so I took the footpath way to work one morning. A herd of young heifers and two horses in the middle field made straight for me as soon as I crossed the stile, no doubt thinking my knapsack contained provender. I could perhaps have dealt with the heifers; but one of the horses, a massive chestnut, insisted on walking close beside me all the way, nudging and nuzzling and trying to eat the knapsack. Then it trod heavily on my shoe. I extricated the foot just in time, and there the creature stood, its great hoof wearing the remains of my shoe. I slapped and shouted, pushed and waved my arms, all to no purpose, and at last had to hop some distance—one foot bare— decoying the horse far enough to allow me to double back and retrieve the shoe, now split right down one side. The other horse and the heifers were, of course, crowding round excitedly to see what would happen next. Fortunately I found a large stick, perhaps left behind by an earlier victim, and by flourishing it at the circus I deterred them for just long enough to reach the next stile without breaking into a run.—*Faith Sharp*

Our Tess
by Winifred Foley

MY sister Tess was so beautiful that at fourteen she could have had the pick of almost any man in the village, eligible or otherwise. She was clever too, but not particularly good. Dad, who was the village carpenter, blacksmith, bee-keeper and counsellor as well as working in the Forest mine, had only to call, 'Where's our Tess?' and she was at his side in a flash, to help turn a chair leg, solder a pit lamp, cut the boys' hair or build a makeshift wireless set. Mam, on the other hand, could 'yell her guts out' for help with black-leading the grate, dusting or washing up, and Tess was as deaf as a door-post. She was the best embroideress in school, the top scholar, and could paint flowers and fruit that would make your nose twitch and mouth water; but rather than darn a hole in the heel of her black woollen stocking she would fold the foot under until it half crippled her to walk. She was Dad's pride and delight, and Mam's constant aggravation.

When she came home for her first fortnight's holiday after a spell in service, the neighbours hardly knew her. Instead of the black button boots and navy serge dress which the packman had been persuaded to let Mam have on tick to equip Tess for starting work, she wore high-heeled court shoes, pink silk stockings, a neat brown suit with *crêpe de Chine* blouse, and dainty gloves to match. Her hair was shingled and waved just like a film star's. Eighteen months of good food, hygiene and money to spend on her person had transformed her out of recognition. Dad cried for joy at seeing her again, and Mam told me to go upstairs and fetch the best cutlery from a shoe-box in her bedroom.

You would have thought that royalty had come to tea.

In her teens Tess had to change jobs frequently, often at the instigation of the mistress when she noticed the way the master's eye kept roving. Sometimes the son of the house or another young relative was seen to be taking too much interest, and that would never do. Tess emerged from these situations more or less intact, with a large collection of signed photographs and love-letters. 'Silly lot o' b——s', she commented kindly, looking at the pinned-up trophies round her bedroom walls. Then during a holiday she met a tall tousle-headed craggy young man from a neighbouring village, a builder employed by a progressive local firm. The attraction was violent and mutual, and in less than a year they were married.

Mon, as she called her husband, was affluent by our standards. They settled in a nice little cottage and, though the children came along in fairly quick succession, they were short of nothing essential except living space. Muddles grew round Tess like tropic vegetation after a monsoon. 'Chuck it behind the sofa', 'Shove it under the table' was her advice to anyone looking for a little spare surface on which to sit. In summer she would pack a basket of food, shut the door on the muddles and take the children for picnics; and on one of these outings they made their way to Waterloo House, a derelict Victorian mansion built by a former squire from the profits of his local coal mine. When the seam gave out he had sacked the men and departed for America to seek new fortunes, and the great house overlooking the slag heap had gradually fallen into neglect.

'What a great gawbee I be!' thought Tess, spreading the picnic on the overgrown lawn while the bigger children clambered about the slag heap looking for

wild strawberries. 'This be the place for us lot.
Plenty o' room for everything.'   She applied her lively
mind to the composing of a suitable letter, and got the
tenancy of the house for a token rent on the understanding that she asked for no repairs.

The move brought out the artist in Tess, and for a
time she scraped and scrubbed, waxed and polished,
papered and painted, forgetting her abhorrence of
housework.   It did not last and the muddles soon
accumulated again, but no matter; if one room over-
flowed they simply moved into another.   Then came
Tess's 'Victorian period'.   The contents of another
big house came under the hammer; Tess went to the
sale and bought, for next to nothing, a load of side-
boards, wardrobes, tables and what-nots, all gigantic
monstrosities.   'Look at all that room in 'em for me
muddles!' she said joyously, and went to more sales.

Despite all the extra wardrobe space, the kitchen
cupboard remained her favourite dumping-ground—
'me filin' cabinet', as she called it.   To open the
bulging plywood doors you had to attack it like a
battering-ram, when it showered forth a miscellany of
objects that defied description.   Rummaging through
it one day, Tess came across the back half of 'Wuthering
Heights', and was soon deep in the stormy life of
Cathy and Heathcliffe.   Fortunately Mon never
minded if a meal was late, knowing that when it did
appear it would be not only excellent but beautifully
served—every dish a work of art, so that he hardly
knew 'whether to yut it or 'ang it on the wall'.

Although he had been brought up by a mother and
sister meticulous in their tidiness, he adapted himself
effortlessly to Tess's chaotic regime.   Rumpled and
relaxed, he ambled about the house like a big good-
natured bear.   He was nudged awake one morning
by Tess and made aware of rain dripping on to her

side of the bed from the leaking roof. 'Muv the bed
to t'other side o' the room', he advised, and went
back to sleep. One day after dinner he settled down
in his old armchair for a doze, the usual Woodbine
in his mouth, the daily paper and the dog Snoozer
on his lap. Tess, in the kitchen, smelt burning and
looked through the glass partition into the dining-room
to see a column of smoke rising out of his chair. 'Wake
up, you ould vool!' she shouted, 'thee chayer's avire!'
Without panic or perceptible movement he slowly
raised an eyelid, then leaned forward carefully so as
not to disturb the sleeping dog, picked up the teapot
from the hearth, poured the remains of the cold tea
on to the smouldering upholstery and resumed his nap.

As the children grew up, married accommodation
was no problem. 'Just clear yerselves out a couple o'
rooms upstairs', offered Tess; and one after another
accepted the invitation, spreading gradually towards
the roof of the big house. Near the top was an
enormous ballroom where dances had been held in the
squire's day. Most of the plaster nymphs had fallen
off the walls, the damp ceiling shed flakes of plaster
and the warped wooden window let in the driving rain.
Reading a farming weekly one day, Tess had another
idea: 'Dip-litter 'ens—that's what I'll kip in there'.
Off she went, bill-hook in hand, to cut quantities of
fern and herbage from the woods for the litter. Mon,
with hardly a fight, produced the money to buy forty
pullets. But they did not take kindly to their aristo-
cratic quarters; they pecked one another's feathers out
and fought like game-birds. 'I know what's the matter
wi' they', said Tess, and went out to buy Farouk, a fine
Rhode Island cockerel. Alas, the next morning when
she went in with their corn, he lay dead in a corner.
'Worked 'isself outa a job, poor sod', she explained.
'Still, 'im 'ad a lovely dyuth.' The hens continued to

peck one another bald. 'Never mind', was Tess's comment. 'Us'll yut the silly b——s, an' they've saved me the job o' pluckin' 'em.'

She has had her share of loss and tragedy, and was never one to take refuge in the consolations of religion. But now that she is a granny many times over, I was not surprised to hear her remark, as she nursed one baby while doing up the shoe-lace of a toddler, 'Well, I must say, thank the Lard I still gotta lot to be thankful for'.

White Cyclamen

OVER leaves, marbled like lizards
　　Or green stones,
Lift probing beaks
That become swans
That become stars
And herds of white horses racing across lichen
And terrible forests, ears laid back, and flaring
Nostrils wide in fear
At the strange far
Journeys, the hoofbeats, the committal.
Day after day
They rear, unfurl, curl, die,
And the wrinkled corm remains, floating like a rhino
Primeval and terrible, harbouring these white
Birds, lizards, horses, stars, as the dark ground
Evolved them, bred them, six million years ago.

Margaret Stanley-Wrench

The Quiet Time of Day
by H. W. Turner

AFTER supper I strolled up the lane to see if Janey was all right. I enjoy a walk in the quiet time of twilight, and the Friesian was due to calve. A cow with good conformation, nice eyes and pleasant expression, she milked quickly and always gave a good yield. She fitted into the herd well, being neither bossy nor afraid, and I liked her. We had a good understanding.

The milking herd was up in the top field. I called it a warm field because it had a gentle slope to the south and the hedges gave good shelter too. The cows liked it and usually calved at the top, where they had burrowed into the hedges. Now, as I opened the gate, all were standing half way up the right-hand side of the field in a semi-circle, facing outwards. I had heard of the protective herd instinct and sometimes seen one or two cows in attendance, but never had I seen the whole herd ranged up in this way. 'That's Jane', I thought.

A calving cow can be an awkward customer. You can side-step a bull, but a cow sights you until the point of impact. If she is tricky it is better to go up on a tractor, or to take a stick and leave the dog behind. A dog infuriates a calving cow and runs to you for protection, so that you are between it and the cow.

I approached quietly and steadily. The cows nearest to me stood absolutely still. I could see Janey now, licking a small calf that stood unsteadily nuzzling at her flank. She lifted her head and mooed very low, looked at me and moved her head slightly. I was about twenty yards away. Then suddenly, at

full speed, she came for me.   Was she looking past me?
I froze and she thundered by like an express train,
only a foot from me, it seemed.   Breathing again, I
turned round to see the farm cat, which must have
followed me up the field, now streaking for home.   I
should have remembered that he liked to accompany
me, though previously he had done so only on sunny
days.

I let Janey return to her calf.   Then I approached
slowly, talking in the way one does: 'Steady, Janey
girl.   What a fine little one you have.   Steady now,
girl.   I'm not going to hurt him'.   A quick check to
see that the calf was all right, iodine on the navel
and a hand to start him sucking.   As I walked away I
could see his tail wagging furiously.   The milk had
come.

Lady into Fox

MY tame fox Agag escaped one October evening and,
being anxious to get him back before the hunt met
the next morning, I decided to wait for him in my field near
his kennel.   I started my vigil at ten o'clock.   It was cold,
wet and windy, so after a time I settled inside the kennel
with a sleeping-bag and pillows and soon went to sleep.
Shortly after 2 a.m. I was wakened by a snuffling sound
and saw Agag's face peeping through the window; but
finding his bed occupied, he darted off again.   Just before
dawn a cold mist came up from the river, and I returned
shivering to the house for a hot drink, then went to my
bedroom for a hot-water bottle.   There was Agag on the
bed, curled up fast asleep on my electric blanket.—*M. M.
Chetham*

'Supposing him to be the gardener': resurrection window at Dulas, Anglesey
by E. Emrys Jones

THE FITTONS OF GAWSWORTH
Dame Alice (above) and Sir Edward were
the parents of Mary (right), maid of
honour to Elizabeth I and a possible
'Dark Lady' of Shakespeare's sonnets.
Several generations of the family are
represented in the church of St James at
Gawsworth, Cheshire. Photographs by
Kennedy McCreadie

Font, probably early Saxon, at Toller Fratrum, Dorset
by J. C. D. Smith

*Font (c. 1150) showing two knights fighting, at Eardisley, Herefordshire
by J. C. D. Smith*

*The Nativity: pulpit panel at Salford Priors, Warwickshire
by J. C. D. Smith*

Adoration of the Magi: alabaster panel from Swansea altarpiece, now in Victoria and Albert Museum, London, by J. C. D. Smith

Detail of slate memorial to William Trebarfoote, Gent. (1628) in Poundstock church, Cornwall, by Leonard and Marjorie Gayton

Our Post Goes Modern
by D. Valley

OURS is a big parish, an isolated geographical
cul de sac, yet only a gentle half hour's drive
from a large town.   We had four or five regular and
part-time carriers of post and a little red van to take
the mail the quarter of a mile from the station to the
post office.   The houses are tucked away down tracks,
behind gates and even across streams, so the postmen
used to walk as the crow flies, through fields and
woods; rarely did they find themselves on the main
road.

For forty years our postman came and went, carrying
the latest local news, stamp books, orders for cherries;
and at Christmas he brought the parcels in his own pony
and trap.   Then the shattering day came when two
men retired and another died.   'The mail's to come
direct by van from town.'   'We'll have to fetch our
own letters.   They'll only deliver on Mondays.'
'Young Jack's to do the lot with the van, and he'll go
on strike.'   The rumours simmered down, and we
heard that 'they' had found three recruits.   Although
we heaved sighs of relief, we still felt sad.   The new
men, we assumed, would be strangers from town—no
more messages and gossip.

On the very day they were appointed, we heard, the
men had laid complaints.   They could all drive, and
all wanted a turn at the van.   The parish was allotted
a small G.P.O. motorcycle to help the van, and our
local postmaster worked out a complicated rota.   As
some routes were easier than others, the men were to
change areas and duties each week.

On the first Monday I went to meet the new man to
explain the intricacies of our gates.   Not until I was

N

half way through my instructions did I realise that the face peering out from the disguising cap belonged to Bill from the garage.   If he did not know how to manage our gate nobody would; after all, he had welded the unique latch himself.   I gaped, embarrassed.   Bill said he was tired of being called out at any hour to mend cars and farm machinery all over the place.   He was glad to take the chance of regular hours and free time he could call his own.

Another new recruit, I was astonished to hear, was Mr Henry, a rather portentous business man who had driven into town and back daily.   He did not drive a Rolls-Royce, but gave that impression.   He was tired of the rat race and had decided to opt out, to follow the quiet life and perhaps do a bit of bird watching when it was not his turn for the van.

The third was Mrs Luxton's Francis.   She had chosen the job for him, not caring for him to do nasty rough farm work; and the big city might lead him astray.   She realised her mistake when she discovered he was walking out with four girls—one in each of his postal areas.

We soon settled into the new routine.   The postmen still do the time-honoured chores, each in his own way. Mr Henry will leave a neat copperplate note to the effect that cabbage plants are for sale at the nursery. Jack will, as usual, forget.   Bill will shout through the kitchen window, and Francis will ring the bell in the hope that my pretty niece will answer the door.   The service continues much as before—sure, if slow.   Last Christmas, a good hour later than usual, I observed Jack's new dog trotting up to our door, followed shortly by the van.

'Do you make your poor dog walk all the way?'   I asked conversationally.

'I 'as to.   I can't 'ave 'un in the van.'

'I suppose he might mess up the letters.'   I marvelled at this unusual adherence to the rules.

'Oh no, 'tain't that.   'E just can't abide travelling. Of course,' he added as one normal dog-lover to another, 'of course, I goes real slow not to tire 'un'.

Historic Building

RIGHT next door to me in Oregon's John Day valley is a solid stone structure, measuring 12 ft by 18 ft, with one door and eight rifle ports.   Ranchers in the valley are in general agreement as to how it came to be there. Shortly after the War between the States a young Captain Magoon, recently discharged from the Confederate cavalry, arrived in the valley on a splendid black stallion.   As an outrider to a wagon train, he had come all the way from Mount Vernon, Virginia, after which the horse was named. A rancher called Jenkins offered to trade the Captain eighty acres of choice valley land for the magnificent animal, which was soon in demand to sire the stocky Indian ponies common in the area.

The high plateau lands were freely roamed by Indians who, along with the coyote, kept vigil over the white man's doings.   Soon Mount Vernon began to disappear on moonless nights, to return a few days later, safe but weary. Jenkins vowed he would put a stop to this and built the fort, which became Mount Vernon's stable.   Each night a ranch hand armed with a rifle was assigned to bunk with the stallion.   During the Indian uprisings in 1868 and 1869 the horse might share his shelter with a dozen or more settlers.   Bullet scars about the rifle ports bear testimony to Indian attempts to breach the fortress.—*Richard Boyd Lawton, Mount Vernon*

Clues to Hardy's Wessex
by Denys Kay-Robinson

WHEN I was invited to tour Thomas Hardy's Wessex and write a book about the changes that have taken place since his day, I did not foresee that I would soon be plunging into a major task of literary-topographical detection. Nearly seventy years have elapsed since Hermann Lea produced the best key to the places hidden under Hardy's fictional names, and I had expected merely to bring it up to date. But I rapidly found myself looking for some of the scenes Lea had left out. I knew the perils of this. When, many years ago, some enthusiasts announced that they had found the village disguised in 'The Woodlanders' as Little Hintock, Hardy not only told them publicly that they were wrong; he said he had spent hours cycling around in a fruitless search for the place himself. But the fascination of the task, as much as the wish to carry out my commission thoroughly, drew me on.

Hardy used every literary device: authentic description, authentic and imaginary mixed, wholly imaginary, buildings and settings transposed to other sites, two real scenes blended into one. An impressive example of the last concerned the mansion Endelstow House in 'A Pair of Blue Eyes', the novel built largely round incidents in the author's own courtship in north Cornwall. The East and West Endelstow of the story are based respectively on St Juliot and Lesnewth, two tiny adjacent villages near Boscastle (Castle Botterel). In truth there is no 'big house' in either, and in one of his prefaces Hardy admitted that the prototype of Endelstow House would have to be 'looked for at a spot several miles south of its supposed site'. Lea failed to identify this correctly, and it was left for F. B. Pinion, in

'A Hardy Companion' (1968), to reveal it as Lanhydrock near Bodmin.

Accordingly with my wife, who did all the driving
and photography, I visited Lanhydrock and found
enough similarities to make its role as the Endelstow
original beyond doubt; but I was puzzled. Endelstow
House had long many-mullioned windows (as did
Lanhydrock), but also

roof lines broken up by dormer lights of the same pattern.
The apex stones of these dormers, together with those of
the gables, were surmounted by grotesque figures in
rampant, passant, and couchant variety. Tall octagonal
and twisted chimneys thrust themselves high up into the
sky, surpassed in height, however, by some poplars and
sycamores at the back . . . In the corners of the court
polygonal bays, whose surfaces were entirely occupied by
buttresses and windows, broke into the squareness of the

Lanhydrock House near Bodmin: a property of the National Trust

enclosure; and a far-projecting oriel, springing from a fantastic series of mouldings, overhung the archway of the chief entrance to the house.

Lanhydrock possessed none of these features. Had Hardy merely invented them or had he, as I suspected, lifted them from some other great house he had seen? After picking out all possible candidates in the county library we sloshed about in pouring rain (*tempo* flaming June) only to find that one after another failed to meet our requirements. We gave up. Hardy must have laid on his own embellishments; after all, he was a trained architect.

Some time later we were visiting Athelhampton, near Puddletown in Dorset, the Athel Hall of two Hardy poems and the short story 'The Waiting Supper'. Suddenly, as we stood in the forecourt, I looked at the house afresh. There before me were mullioned dormers with gables and curious finials, similar finials on the roof gables and, in the angle of the building, a polygonal bay that was all buttresses and windows. Behind a tall ornate chimney and the roof rose taller trees. All that was lacking was the oriel. Much interested, Athelhampton's owner, Robert Cooke, M.P., went inside and presently emerged with a large picture. It showed the old gatehouse, now demolished; and over the gate a splendid oriel rose from a series of mouldings truly 'fantastic'.

I was then taken to a workshop in which the stones of the oriel, carefully numbered, lay awaiting recon- struction elsewhere in the grounds. As a young man Hardy knew Athelhampton well; in fact he had painted a watercolour of it (but with the oriel hidden) that now hangs in the Dorset County Museum. So he had created his Endelstow House in north Cornwall from a mansion in the south of the county, and enlivened it with features from one in Dorset.

Athelhampton House: old print showing former gatehouse

Occasionally I was helped by letters or memoirs of Hardy's friends published since Lea wrote, but more often my detective achievements were simply the result of carefully re-reading Hardy's clues, comparing them with what I could see in the field and questioning local people, especially those whose recollections stretched back half way or more to the days about which Hardy mostly wrote.

At times we lacked even a fictitious name on which to base questions, as with the nameless weir beside which the old drunkard drowned in the short story 'A Tragedy of Two Ambitions'. From the use in the tale of some already identified Hardy names, and even a single real one, it had been established that the setting lay in either East or West Coker near Yeovil, and that the weir was somewhere along the little stream which runs through them. The weir itself was held to be imaginary, but I saw no reason why it should be.

Until the present century even the tiniest streams abounded in mills, each with at least one weir near by. The weir in the story had a footbridge, carrying a path-way over it, and adjoined a narrow culvert under a bridge for wagons to enter the meadow.   Not far off stood the local manor (Narrobourne House), its lights visible at night from the weir.   We noted from period maps the position of every mill and weir in the two parishes and proceeded to do the rounds.   Like the Cornish man-sions, one after another proved to be a disappointment. We could see from the sites that even those which had been demolished would not have been right.

We had almost reached the end of the list when, up a little *cul-de-sac* in the hamlet of Holywell, between the two Cokers, we came on a layout so perfectly answering to Hardy's picture that the case for its having been his model could not be stronger.   The sole objection was that West Coker Manor was farther away across the meads than the narrative implied; but, with so many other features fitting into place, we did not feel we were forcing the evidence by assuming that here Hardy was doing a little transposing to suit his tale.   Our dis-covery was only just in time; the weir remains, but the culvert and wagon bridge have been replaced by a stone-and-concrete structure.

Both as poet and as novelist he evidently had a high regard for milestones, which appear in many of his works.   Most of those removed in 1939 for reasons of security have been reinstated; but some were buried and others stored, and their precise whereabouts for-gotten.   By good fortune I managed to trace two missing Hardy stones, one in each category.

Following the Puddletown (Weatherbury) road out of Dorchester I had no difficulty in observing the first stone, on which Henchard, the fallen Mayor of Caster-bridge, had rested his basket on his exit to obscurity;

nor the second, against which the dying Fanny Robin
had leaned on her journey to the Union. But where
was the third, featured in the delicious poem 'The Milestone by the Rabbit-Burrow'? It should have been
where the road runs through Yellowham (Yalbury,
Yell'ham) Wood, roughly opposite the track to Keeper
Day's House of 'Under the Greenwood Tree' fame.

'Buried in 1939,' said the county surveyor, 'and
no-one knows where'. It happened that I had still to
call on the successor to Keeper Day, and I mentioned
the milestone. 'It's buried all right,' he said, 'and I
watched them bury it. I know exactly where it is, but
the council people have never consulted me'. I have
not passed on the news yet.

The other is the most famous of Hardy's milestones,
on the road from Fawley (Marygreen) to Wantage
(Alfredston), on the back of which the young Jude the
Obscure cut his symbol of hope before going to Oxford
(Christminster) and disillusionment. I found that the
stones along the main road had been replaced, apart
from the three nearest to Wantage; and I needed the
nearest but one. In this area the local authority had
collected and stored its stones; and by a piece of luck
I made inquiries just as they had found the three missing
ones under a pile of debris in the council yard. The
stones were stood up for me to see; and so vivid is that
most powerful of all Hardy's novels, I felt half convinced
that, if I could have looked behind the granite monster,
traces of Jude's handiwork would have met my eyes.
Of course, not all my attempts to fill in the gaps left
by Hermann Lea were so successful. Some ended in
tantalising uncertainty, others in complete frustration.

One mystery we encountered was not of Hardy's
creation. In 'The Trumpet-Major' a scene is laid in
a granary built on staddle-stones, somewhere on the
chalk downs north-east of Weymouth. No staddle-

Author (l.) *standing by three missing milestones in council yard*

built structures remain in this area, but we knew there were a few elsewhere in Wessex. We had not yet sought one to photograph when, returning home one evening through Hazelbury Bryan (Hardy's Nuttlebury) in central Dorset, we both saw a splendid wooden building on close-set staddles beside the road.

It was still light enough for us not to be using headlamps, but we preferred to leave camera-work until our next visit to the area, which took place a few weeks later. But where was our building? Our recollections of it agreed: it stood in a dip, at a curve of the road so that it faced us as we approached, and there had been other buildings beside and opposite it. We combed the rather scattered village, we asked at the store, the Antelope, various farmhouses, the home of the local wiseacre. Not only did people not know of any such structure standing; they could recall none.

We searched in widening circles for miles around. The only building on staddles, at a distant farm, was half the size of ours, on fewer and taller stones. Yet I am positive we were driving through Hazelbury Bryan that evening; I wrote an entry in my notebook on the spot. Perhaps, if Thomas Hardy could return for a moment, I might present him with a conundrum for a change.

Then There Were Five

BY the time the corn was ripe in the field adjoining our garden we were overrun with rabbits. Our kitchen garden had taken a beating, and rose trees were cropped to the ground. It was obvious we would have to get rid of the marauders, though I found the young ones distinctly appealing. Untouched by fear, a family would wander up to the rose bed, reach up like tiny kittens for the blooms and nibble them off with alacrity and delight when I was within a foot of them. The farmer started combining, and a friend offered his services as a second gun. My husband and I asked if we might have some corn for the harvest festival and were generously left enough for half a dozen stooks, to be cut by hand, round the stalwart oak in the centre of the field. When the combine left, only five rabbits had fallen to the guns; the rest had slipped into nettlebeds bordering the dell. We made our way gingerly across the stubble to the oak before the sparrows could strip the ears. At the first sweep of the scythe a fox, vixen and three cubs loped off to cover with easy grace. The farmer was astonished to hear this when he visited us later. But we were all reduced to laughter, for out on the front lawn a huge doe rabbit with four young ones was placidly cropping the grass under our very noses.—*Margaret Hubball*

Death on the Ice
by William A. Woodrow

THREE days and nights of frost had sealed the drains and flashes of the Norfolk marsh. The tidal river had coated fringes and fronds of vegetation, looking like crystallised angelica. The ice was thickest in the cutting up to the boat-house, where I broke it twice a day and scattered corn so that the waterfowl might come to feed in relative safety. The boat-house itself provided an excellent hide. It was a regular feature of the landscape and therefore inconspicuous; it offered protection from the bone-splitting east wind and gave me a good view of the birds which flocked to the spot. These were mainly moorhens, mallard and teal with an occasional coot and once a great crested grebe. But I was too visible; in spite of their hunger the birds were wary, and any sound, amplified in that still frosty air, sent them off at once. Unlike wild geese, they did not keep a watchman. All seemed to feed avidly, yet at a signal unnoticed by me they would disperse on the instant, the duck flying off, the coots and moorhens waddling away to the river's open water.

A slight chill kept me indoors for a night and a day while it continued to freeze. After tea I wrapped up and went out again with a crowbar; as I expected, the cutting was frozen over. What I did not expect, though I had heard of its happening, was to see a bird captured by the ice. It was a teal, held by legs and tail feathers, and it seemed to be dead. In the shadow of the boat-house I wondered what to do; the ice was too thin to bear me. Then I heard a high-pitched squeaking from the reeds, like an unoiled brake or mice in the walls of an old cottage. It went on and on until the withered stems parted and a weasel writhed out into the open. It stepped daintily, sniffed the air, paused, looked behind for an instant, then lunged its head and neck forward towards the captive teal. Two others followed.

Warily the three tiny creatures came to the cutting's edge. The leader touched the ice with a tentative paw and drew back. It moved forward again cautiously on to the surface, followed by the other two. They had obviously scented the teal and hunger drew them on. As, with a curious weaving side-stepping gait, they came nearer, the teal moved. Fear had conquered exhaustion, and it made frantic efforts to pull free.

Not more than two feet from the bird the first weasel suddenly reared up, quite vertical, sitting on its tail like an otter. Once more came the quiet squeaking as it began to weave about, with head, shoulders and forepaws all moving. The others, about two feet behind, began to mimic this, but neither was able to stay erect with the same freedom and grace. On all fours again, the weasels began to circle clockwise round the teal, then stopped. More weaving before they reversed and ran counter-clockwise. They stopped, weaved and reversed again and again until a definite rhythm was built up. This seemed to hypnotise the teal; it gave up tugging at the ice and sat, beak agape, rotating its head as the weasels ran around and about it.

Suddenly they all halted, as if some silent signal had passed, and retreated almost to the edge of the cutting where they lay flat, their russet coats contrasting with the leaden colour of the ice. The leader began to work forwards again, while the other two lay watching. The teal watched too, but exhaustion overcame it once more and it gradually sank on to the ice. Nearer came the weasel until almost within touch. Then it reared up on its tail, slowly this time, and the teal rose with it, until the two creatures, the tiny predator and the much larger bird, were both at full stretch and facing each other. The weasel darted, caught the teal by the throat and the two collapsed together. Again the impression of a silent signal and the other weasels pounced. Between them they tore the teal from the ice. The leader gripped it and with a curious shake, like a dog with a rabbit or an old glove, dragged the prey off into the reeds, followed by the others.

Jim Vincent, formerly gamekeeper on the Horsey estate, a few miles to the north, told me that he had once seen weasels take a teal in a hard winter before the war. But the interest lies not so much in the unusual prey as in the reason for their behaviour in the preliminary stages. They may have been carrying out a sequence that is part of the ritual of the kill. Once started, they were virtually unable to change it, because it is a genetically determined pattern for weasels on the hunt. There are other interpretations. The most likely is that the weasels, facing a situation outside their normal experience, had to improvise a plan of campaign and were working themselves up to a pitch at which they could attack their large prey with impunity.

KITTEN'S CRECHE. A friend's cat produced one kitten in the potting shed about a hundred yards from the house. As a rule she would not let it out of her sight, but whenever she wanted a night out she would meow at the back door, march in with the kitten and wait until it was comfortably settled on lap or cushion. Then she would demand to be let out again, returning early next morning to collect the kitten and carry it back to the shed.—*E. Ann Howes*

Tail Corn

A little measly talk over neighbours is right enough; it do make the day go by a little quicker and sends a body to bed with a chuckle—Mrs Ellis's 'Villager'

NORTH RIDING farmer, concluding sale of second-hand car: 'Tha's got a reight bargain 'ere, lad. There's money on t' windscreen'—tapping the unexpired licence—'an' what's more'—pointing to the tyres—'it's got reight good booits on'.

WEST SOMERSET farm worker tinkering with motorcycle: ' 'Er doan't rattle proper'.

CHESHIRE woman customer to shopkeeper inquiring after her mother: 'She's very well, but now she's ninety-one we don't think it's safe for her to go shopping on her bike, so we've bought her a horse instead'.

YORKSHIRE dalesman, regretting ill-considered action: 'Ah've rued ivery hair of me heead'.

NORFOLK farmer: 'Sheep don't want to hear the church bells ring in the same pasture twice—can't abide the taste of their own smell'.

CO. ARMAGH woman, of old father devotedly sitting with stricken wife: 'He's just like a clockin' hen with her'.

SURREY cottager, asked name of fine bush in her garden: 'A flowering primus'.

HARASSED housewife, struggling to get husband's meal in time: 'Gawd help them that has to make mate [meat] by the bell'.

YORKSHIRE woman, of lazy daughter: 'Ah said to 'er, "If you'd nobbut tidy your spot ivery day, you wouldn't 'ev ti di it sea often", but she disn't tak' a bit o' notice'.

NORTHUMBRIAN villager at post office: 'I wants one o' they envelopes that you lap o'er an' clag doon'.

OLD DEVON widower, asked how he was managing for meals: 'Oh, I lives next to Fred [another widower], an' when I 'as meat an' tetties 'e comes in to I, an' when 'e 'as meat an' tetties I guz in to 'e'.

A guinea is offered for the best paragraph; it must be true and original.   Also-rans, if printed, earn the usual rate.   This quarter the guinea goes to R. K. Forster for the first.

New Books about the Country

I rejoice to concur with the common reader, for by the common sense of readers, uncorrupted by literary prejudices, after all the refinements of subtilty and the dogmatism of learning, must be generally decided all claims—*Johnson*

The Sense of Place

AN honoured line of writers —Wordsworth, Ruskin, Morris, Cyril Joad, Clough Williams-Ellis and Ian Nairn among them—have over the years inveighed against the ravaging of Britain's landscape. Their emphasis has been on the impact of railway development, industry, urban sprawl, cars and 'things in fields' on the land. In THE ASSAULTS ON OUR SENSES (Methuen, 50s) *John Barr* gives the subject a new and possibly fruitful twist—the impact which man's abuse of the land has on man himself. Our eyes, ears, noses, taste and touch are all being abused by rural and urban squalor, by ever-growing traffic, by noise of all kinds, by pollution of land, air and water, by 'man-handled food', by plastic products. This abuse is justified by many as part of the price of progress, in spite of the increasingly clear connexion between all forms of pollution on the one hand and physical sickness, psychological stress and high costs in lost production or land maintenance on the other.

John Barr ends with a strong plea for continued and extended Government action to control all forms of pollution, and for greater public awareness of the damage to us and to the land. One strong thrust towards such action and such awareness must come from what Cyril Joad called the 'townsman's invasion of the countryside'; in LAND AND LEISURE (D. & Charles, 84s) *J. Allan Patmore* brings together as no-one has before many of the facts and ideas in this vital field. With masses of figures and maps, he describes the enormous post-war growth in demand for almost all outdoor leisure activities, emphasising the wide variety of activities desired—and hence of facilities needed—from play spaces to golf courses, footpaths to water-ski areas. He high-lights the paradox that man, in his search for rural peace and beauty, can damage those very qualities; and he shows how we have been forced to move from strict preservation to active management of coasts, inland waters, forests, common lands and many other resources. A most useful book, with ample references.

The desire of the townsman to understand the countryside, and the growing importance of the countryside also as a living subject of study in our schools, are already reflected in a wide range of books. For the general reader they include the excellent series of National Park guides, published by H.M.S.O. for the Countryside Commission, of which the latest is EXMOOR NATIONAL PARK, edited by *John Coleman-Cooke* and very good value at 8s 6d; and also the Hodder and Stoughton series on 'The Making of the English Landscape', of which *Arthur Raistrick's* WEST RIDING OF YORKSHIRE (40s) forms a worthy third volume.

For the more specialist reader, and particularly for field work by students, the Blandford Press has produced the third book in its series GEOGRAPHY THROUGH FIELDWORK, by *T. Bolton* and *P. A. Newbury* (21s). It has compact and meaty chapters on eight areas, rural and urban, with a significant and stimulating emphasis on in-dustrial archaeology. 'The Dalesman' has issued LAKELAND LANDSCAPE, by *J. C. Barringer* (16s), based on exploration by parties from Lancaster Royal Grammar School, where he teaches.

All these books may enhance the reader's sense of place, while giving him information. A more direct intent to invoke the sense of place, indeed the very symbolism of landscape, animates a cerebral book by *G. A. Jellicoe*, STUDIES IN LANDSCAPE DESIGN—3 (O.U.P., 65s). He is a well-known landscape architect, and this rather elusive book contains a set of talks or reports he has prepared in recent years. The most interesting are those in which he relates the work of sculptors and painters to that of landscape architects, and shows how the simple geometry of circles, squares and crosses can be combined with a sense of place to produce strong landscape.—*Michael Dower*

Occupational Hazards

THE need to penetrate the uniqueness and individuality of a certain place at a certain moment in time has always challenged both artist and writer. The village, particularly, offers a seductive mixture of matter-of-factness and mystery which both fascinates and frustrates the newcomer; for there can be no final con-clusion. *Geoffrey Grigson*, combining a rare degree of acerbity, rural learning and poetry, describes his encounter with a French village called Trôo in NOTES FROM AN ODD COUNTRY (Macmillan, 50s). It is the poet Ronsard's homeland, a country of the mind as well as of the grape. Scrawled by centuries of ploughs, scarred

by pagan and Christian cruel-
ties, alternately cursed and
blessed, it is both every village
in Europe and yet subtly itself:
field work, limitation, art,
human endurance, God and
politics; the blueness of the
river and Morning Glory, of
the southern sky and the
shadows on the Roman road.
This is a wonderful attempt by
a stranger, courteously though
determinedly, to find his way
to the heart of things.

A fresh selection of *Thomas
Hardy's* STORIES AND
POEMS has been edited by
Donald J. Morrison (Dent,
18s). Hardy, who said that his
business was to 'show the
sorriness underlying the grand-
est things, and the grandeur
underlying the sorriest things',
is represented here by tales
which link the grim rural
England of George IV's time—
a period which haunted Hardy
—to the early 20th century.
Here too are those marvellous
and overwhelming poems he
wrote in 1912 after the death of
his first wife, and in which he
triumphantly overcomes the
tragedy of the marriage. His
villagers and peasant soldiers
struggle along in what he calls
'a nonchalant universe'. He is
the poet of helplessness, and
this excellent volume offers a
powerful introduction to his
world.

With   MALTAVERNE
(Eyre, 35s) *François Mauriac*,
who died earlier this year,

returned to the country he
knew as a boy. This is the
region around Bordeaux, a
broad and lonely area known
as the Landes which, with its
pines, light soil and marshes, is
not unlike the Suffolk sand-
lings. It is a story about
adolescence during the ten-
sions caused by the great
quarrel between Church and
State in France at the turn of
the century. Two friends, a
peasant seminarist and an in-
tellectual from the local
château, struggle to free themselves from crippling customs,
only to suffer that intense
guilt which is peculiar to
French Catholics, and which is
the basis of so much drama in
French literature. This is a
brilliant novel about early love,
class, the mind and God. The
period, 1902-07, is perfectly
evoked.

In   COLERIDGE   AND
WORDSWORTH IN SOM-
ERSET (D. & Charles, 50s)
Berta Lawrence has succeeded in
gazetteering the beginning of
the Romantic Movement in
England. By a series of co-
incidences stemming from college friendships, a group of
young men, with their wives
and sisters and all in their
twenties, found themselves in
the Quantocks. There, among
suspicious locals, government
spies (the second Napoleonic
war was in full swing), two of
the friends produced a book
which changed the direction of

English poetry. This delightful well-illustrated volume gives a lane - by - lane, cottage - by cottage and almost a meal-by-meal account of what happened during the days when 'Lyrical Ballads' was being written.

'Within the covers of this book are almost all the short stories about birds, animals and fish I wrote in my youth', says *Henry Williamson* in his introduction to COLLECTED NATURE STORIES (Macdonald, 40s). He does not mention that also within these same covers, unconscious almost and only incidental to the main theme, is one of the most remarkable descriptions of village life immediately following the 1914-18 war. Here is the West Country, rough and undiscovered, ignorant, beautiful and strange in its neglect. Here too is a first-hand account of the old village poverty. Where the creatures are concerned, the most tender friendships and blood sports fuse in a long and exquisitely detailed agenda of living and dying, loving and killing, nursing and slaughter.

Sterling North has written a novel based on the friendship which began when his father, then a boy, met the Swedish-American naturalist Thure Kumlien. It is a simple frontier tale of the 1870s, full of American innocence. The boy crosses the boundary which divides the law of a puritan deity from the law of the wilderness. THE WOLFLING (Heinemann, 30s) is attractively written and sensitively illustrated, and would have a particular appeal for 12- to- 16-year-olds.

GREEN HERB FOR MEAT (Collins, 30s) is one of the first novels to deal intelligently with the economic realities of the present farming crisis. *Harold Geach* sets his story about the traditional farmer and the new arable and animal tycoons in East Anglia, where big business is creating moral and social problems in the villages. He writes with unusual knowledge of the changing scene and skilfully avoids the sentimentality which such a theme suggests. A dramatic picture of the rural John Wilders *versus* the rest.

Ian Niall's writing is deservedly famous for its fine restraint; he is a master of the rural understatement. THE GALLOWAY SHEPHERD (Heinemann, 42s) is a tale about a young 'herd' who builds up a fine flock from scratch in the Scottish hills. It does not try to devalue the idyllic quality of this kind of sheep farming, but does emphasise its loneliness—even its unnaturalness, for it draws a man into great solitudes. Until the day arrives when sheep leave the hills for the factory farm, this is how it must always be—a biblical or classical experience going on above the motorways.

Every bit as much a text-book as yet another leaf from *Arthur Randell's* macabre auto-biography, FENLAND MOLE-CATCHER (Routledge, 21s) is about his and his ancestors' long tradition of vermin ex-termination—a necessary task which does not make a pretty story. A quietly factual East Anglian voice runs a bloody circle round the grudged lives of rat, mouse, hare, weasel, fox, marten, hedgehog, pigeon, sparrow, magpie, finch and mole. How easy to telephone Pest Control! How hard to read what happens next!

It struck me, after reading *W. J. Lewis's* intriguing account of his 33 years in the light-house service, that he had endured most of the emotions of imprisonment except dis-grace. CEASELESS VIGIL (Harrap, 26s) is full of excep-tional observation of the marine life which clings to lighthouses and their wild bases, and of the busy ritualistic existence which goes on inside the flashing tower. Yet melancholy in-vades all. It is not an unlik-able quality: in fact, by its very existence it turns what might otherwise have been yet one more interesting account of an unusual occupation into something quite extraordinary. There is 'Providence' caring for those inside, and the seals 'weeping like children' outside. There is either a terrible silence or an appalling noise. There is also the glimpse of ordinary working men be-coming contemplatives.—
Ronald Blythe

Infinite Riches

THE WHAT TO SEE ATLAS of England, Wales and Northern Ireland, pub-lished for the National Trust by Index at 35s, is a brilliant idea as well as remarkable value for money. Historic buildings, landscapes, gardens, outstanding villages, bridges, wind and water mills and other industrial monuments are numbered on each map and identified by an accompanying gazetteer—a stock-list of in-finite riches and a topographical catalogue which all the books here noticed illuminate in their very different ways. This fifth edition of the atlas, first pub-lished in 1964, includes a number of additional refer-ences.

For the curious, THE NAMES OF TOWNS AND CITIES OF BRITAIN (Bats-ford, 50s) is a necessary adjunct to any atlas. *Dr Margaret Gelling* and *Professors Melville Richards* and *W. F. H. Nicolaisen*, who have been responsible for the English, Welsh and Scot-tish names respectively, have compiled what the publishers claim to be the first comprehensive book on place-name derivation to appear for 60 years. The book is fascinating to dip into, but the choice of names is capricious rather than comprehensive.

THE EARTHEN LONG BARROW IN BRITAIN, by *Paul Ashbee* (Dent, 6 gns), is a meticulous study of its subject, sumptuously produced with numerous photographs and site plans. Although intended primarily for archaeologists, it will interest all who find these lonely burial places of neolithic man strangely evocative. But a word of warning to the layman: a review in a distinguished contemporary described this book as a definitive work on the long barrow, whereas (as the author makes clear on the very first page) the term 'earthen' specifically excludes the stone-chambered long barrows of which Belas Knap and Hetty Pegler's Tump on the Cotswolds are notable examples.

Those who enjoy the pastime of 'church crawling' when exploring the countryside, however minimal their knowledge of the architecture, often suppose that Saxon remains are extremely rare. They will be disabused, and their journeys in Sussex vastly enriched, by THE SAXON CHURCHES OF SUSSEX, by *E. A. Fisher* (D. & Charles, 63s). He describes and illustrates no fewer than 60 churches which reveal evidence — sometimes substantial—of Saxon origin. The reason for this unusually high rate of survival was the isolation of the county by forest and marsh which made it for long accessible only by sea or from the west.

Eric Delderfield is a well-known authority on the topography of the South-West, and in WEST COUNTRY HISTORIC HOUSES AND THEIR FAMILIES, Vol. 2 (D. & Charles, 50s) he presents finely illustrated descriptions of 21 subjects in Dorset, Wiltshire and North Somerset, ranging from small medieval manors like Bolehyde in Wiltshire to great Palladian mansions such as Stourhead. No less fascinating are his accounts of the people who have lived in them over the years. The fact that all but three of the properties are still in private hands will hearten those who deplore the passing of the English country house.

The well-illustrated BRIDGES IN BRITAIN, by *G. Bernard Wood* (Cassell, 42s), is a gossipy folk-lory book. It has little to say about the development of bridge engineering or the particular problems encountered in construction. Curiously the canal builders, who were responsible for hundreds of simple but beautiful bridges which now grace the English scene, receive scant mention. Only Telford's great aqueduct at Pont Cysyllte, which is atrociously mis-spelt, gets a mention.

Alan Bloom is a man of parts: not only an enterprising and expert nurseryman who has written several gardening books, but also a steam enthusiast. In 1947 he acquired a Burrell traction engine to do odd jobs on his new farm at Bressingham in Norfolk. 'Bella', as he called her, was the foundation stone of a live steam museum, an attraction that now draws thousands from all over the country. In STEAM ENGINES AT BRESSINGHAM (Faber, 50s) he tells the story of his collection and individual exhibits. Finely illustrated in colour and half-tone, it is a 'must' for anyone whose nose twitches at the scent of hot cylinder oil.

My first choice among this quarter's books is MR LOUDON'S ENGLAND, by *John Gloag* (Oriel, 50s), a biography of absorbing interest to which it is impossible to do justice briefly. Landscape gardener, author and architect, John Claudius Loudon (1783-1843) was a man of extraordinary energy and versatility who probably had a greater influence on the Victorian domestic scene than any other man of his generation. The plane trees in London's squares owe their origin to Loudon, his designs for glass-houses inspired Joseph Paxton and, as the many period illustrations reproduced from his architectural 'Encyclopaedia' reveal, the Victorian suburban house in all its eclectic variety was based on Loudon's prototypes.

Finally two reprints of more than usual historical interest and flavour. First the 1858 OFFICIAL ILLUSTRATED GUIDE TO THE SOUTH EASTERN RAILWAY AND ITS BRANCHES, by *George Meason* (E. & W. Books, 3 gns). This is a facsimile reproduction of a charming, copiously illustrated example of railway topographical writing by an author who (to quote his own preface), 'from practical experience, is enabled to retain the prominent position he has held so long as a railway topographer, notwithstanding the feeble attempts of similar rival publications to compete with his own'.

BICYCLING 1874: A Text Book for Riders (D. & Charles, 30s) is a splendid period piece from the days when intrepid men on their solid-tyred penny-farthings were rediscovering the roads of England, which had been neglected since railways eclipsed the stage coach. How appallingly bad our roads then were may be gathered from the touring itineraries. As they pedalled indomitably onward over surfaces 'very rutty and uneven' or 'three inches deep in mud', they can hardly have realised that they were blazing a trail which the motor car would soon follow.— *L. T. C. Rolt*

Travellers All

IF threats to the British countryside show few signs of decreasing, neither does the number of defenders anxious to describe its past history and present attractions. Here are six books by travellers who have chosen to eulogise particular areas, all full of information, with adequate maps and good black-and-white photographs. *John Seymour's* THE COMPANION GUIDE TO EAST ANGLIA (Collins, 45s) has some striking illustrations; the unexpected phrase or word enlivens his text, a splendid collection of facts about past and present from Roman bricks to a fibre-glass dove, from old statues and paintings to the name of the custodian at a stately home. The arrangement is in regions, place by place, with advice on how to get from one to the other. Place-names are in heavy type, and there are useful chapters

Wendens Ambo, Essex, by Stanley Bond

on the coast, hotels, bird-watching and the East Anglian dialect.

J. R. L. Anderson's THE UPPER THAMES (Eyre, 75s) takes the history of the whole area up to Norman times, then follows the record of the river and its towns, its tributaries and their settlements, and ends with a survey of modern times, including the Harwell atomic research establishment. A very brief gazetteer gathers up all the towns and villages.

HERTFORDSHIRE, by *W. Branch Johnson* (Batsford, 30s), has a similar and equally readable approach—a slice of history with local illustrations. Chapters cover roads, towns, castles and churches, leaving the reader to find his own routes and explore for himself. The county has for centuries been a home for wealthy Londoners, and is today an 'intimate mingling of rural past and sophisticated present' with 65 per cent of the total acreage still devoted to agriculture.

Subject by subject, not island by island, is how *Raoul Lemprière* paints his PORTRAIT OF THE CHANNEL ISLANDS (Hale, 30s), describing the roads, then the famous people, the past, the law, the buildings and agriculture, right down to details of stamps, coins, cere-monies and local dishes: all of great interest to those who follow in his footsteps.

I found *Harry J. Scott's* YORKSHIRE HERITAGE (Hale, 30s) less methodical, but more entertaining. He begins with a picture of the county and its people as portrayed by novelists and writers, then describes his own journeys along the highways, down the coast, among the old buildings and industries, moving nimbly from century to century as the fancy takes him, and discussing human beings, their activities and the memorials they leave behind them.

THE SUNSET COASTS by *Vivian Bird* (Roundwood, 35s), is a chatty book about touring up the west coast of Ireland to the Hebrides, Orkney and Shetland, accom-panied part of the way by his family. The things he finds continually remind him of other trips and of information which he readily imparts to the reader.—*Margaret Campbell*

The Days That Are No More

' A QUIET group of genuine seekers into the past' aptly describes these five books. The original reference was to people like *A. K. Hamilton* *Jenkin*, for whose volume 'Cornish Seafarers' Arthur Quiller-Couch was writing an introduction. 'Cornwall and the Cornish' and 'Cornish

Homes and Customs' completed the survey of this corner of Celtic Britain, and now we have a new edition of the composite work, CORNWALL AND ITS PEOPLE (D. & Charles, 84s). Reality and romance jostle significantly; wreckers and smugglers were ill-paid fishermen and miners, not swashbucklers; witchcraft taboos were matched by hell-fire Methodism and Sunday school treats; and, rather than quaintness, it is the rural calendar that dictates observances, food and pastimes.

COTSWOLD GAMES (Tabard, 2 gns) is a facsimile reprint of the 1878 copy of 'Annalia Dubrensia', a collection of poems — including Drayton's and Johnson's—published in 1636 to celebrate the 'yeerely Olympicks' to afford 'harmless mirth and jollitie'. The founder, Robert Dover, is hailed in heroic verse for promoting football, horse-racing, bell-ringing, cock-fighting, dancing, quoits and other sports. Stratford was but ten miles away, and Shakespeare alludes to the meetings as if he had witnessed them. They continued 'with great spirit' until 1851 when, as the editor E. R. *Vyvyan* put it in the preface, decorum was replaced by 'license and impropriety . . . all sorts of disturbances . . . demoralising the whole neighbourhood', and an Act of Parliament stopped them.

The familiar echo is sounded again by *Master William Morris*, a local journalist, who included a chapter in SWINDON (Tabard, 70s) to illustrate the need for a Reform Bill because elections in the 1800s caused drunkenness, riots, immorality and debauchery. His thick book is reprinted — another facsimile—from the original of 1885 with the subtitle, 'Reminiscences, Notes and Relics of Ye Old Wiltshire Towne'. It is a prodigious social document too, despite the avowed aim to preserve and amuse instead of lecture and instruct, with a range embracing architecture, Flemish cloth-workers, dame schools, rioting labourers, mummers, wells and wagons.

The last were not for THE DROVERS (Macmillan, 55s), who performed feats of endurance on their own two legs as they and their faithful dogs moved cattle, sheep and poultry from the lonely farms to the markets. Before the Industrial Revolution brought roads, canals and railways, the daily hazards along the rough tracks included storm, flood and thief. In extended research *K. J. Bonser* has traced the history of an epoch which ended with the hundredth birthday of the last drover in 1961, having started in the grassy uplands of Britain 6000 years ago.

With more clearings in the lowland forests, farming proper began; and the Roman invaders further improved agriculture. At this point *T. K. Butcher* takes up the story in COUNTRY LIFE (Batsford, 20s), a handsome picture-book to illumine such themes as Saxons and Normans, life at the manor, Tudors and Stuarts, the squire and the parish poor, corn laws and trade unions. The stress of towns is turning men's thoughts to the peace and pursuits of their ancestors minus the poverty, but no rampant nostalgia mars the message of these books. The author sums it up when he says that 'compromise has to be reached between the unchanging picture-postcard village and the sprawling dormitory'.—*Grace Banyard*

A Gardener's Library

A NEW edition of *W. J. Bean's* TREES AND SHRUBS HARDY IN THE BRITISH ISLES is an event for all keen gardeners, since it has become one of our standard reference works. Volume One (Murray, 160s) which takes us only from A to C, has been revised by a distinguished team under Sir George Taylor, Director of Kew; but it is to the industry and knowledge of Desmond Clarke that we mainly owe it, and the work is well done. There will be four—this first, including some preliminary chapters, has grown to 845 pages—and the whole will probably be the most thorough book on its subject available anywhere in the world. Its particular value for gardeners lies in the little notes, at the end of each description, on the plant's size and behaviour in gardens. It is astonishing how large some of the comparatively recent introductions of Forrest and Kingdon Ward have grown, and the notes have required considerable revision. Bean's original descriptions were written, with great experience and knowledge, largely from living material and most of them have stood the test of time, though there have been too many changes of nomenclature. This monumental work is to be relied on, and I can only commend it, without attempted criticism, to 'Countryman' readers.

Tyler Whittle's THE PLANT HUNTERS: 3450 Years of Searching for Green Treasure (Heinemann, 55s) is a fascinating complement to Bean's work. It is an erudite book, but also highly entertaining and written with great verve. The author starts with Queen Hatshepsut in ancient Egypt; she sent a successful expedition to the land of Punt (probably Somaliland) to bring back frankincense trees, and she did it in style with five ships. He ends with George Forrest in Western China and on the borders of Tibet. He ran, alone and bleeding, for eight days before a fanatical gang of Tibetans; yet he survived to gather more than 31,000 specimens and to introduce probably more good garden plants than any other collector.

I suppose that most gardens owe more than half their plants to the collectors, but the remainder derive from the breeder's intuitive skill, so the other complement to Bean is THE DEVELOPMENT OF GARDEN FLOWERS, by *Richard Gorer* (Eyre, 63s). He deals briefly with the main principles of plant breeding and then gives us chapters on individual flowers, tracing their development to their present size of flower, variety of colour and garden value. It is an interesting story, slightly different in each genus, largely relying on intelligent guesswork of probabilities in the early days, since there are no records. The book is well illustrated with drawings from the 'Botanical Magazine', the Reeves collection of Chinese drawings at the Royal Horticultural Society and other old books.

From the hunt for plants and their development we pass readily to the gardens in which they grow, and many readers as well as gardeners will welcome the new cheaper edition of GREAT GARDENS OF BRITAIN, by *Peter Coats* (Spring Books, 59s), first published in 1967. It is wonderful value, and some of the photographs both in colour and in black-and-white are magnificent. The author has chosen 38 fine gardens—most of them open to the public—of great and spacious houses and gives a brief description, lavishly illustrated, of each.

Harry Wheatcroft is a real enthusiast for roses, especially the hybrid teas and floribundas, and he tells of his life with them in a book he describes as 'notes on a love affair'. IN PRAISE OF ROSES (Barrie, 40s) is certainly entertaining, and somewhat flamboyant, as well as informative. Harry introduced to England, though he did not raise, four of our best and most popular roses: Peace, Super Star, Queen Elizabeth and Fragrant Cloud. He tells of the big industry rose growing has become, and gives us his valuable assessment of many of the newer roses with his selection.

In WOODLAND PLANTS AND SUN LOVERS (Faber, 50s) *Harold and Joan Bawden* record those which have done well for them. These personal books by skilled gardeners are valuable because they are based on hard experience. The directions for planting are good and precise. A number of unusual plants are included, so there is something here for all kinds of gardeners.

Another personal book, and one that I recommend particularly as a present for a discriminating gardener, is *Christopher Lloyd's* THE WELL-TEMPERED GARDEN (Collins, 50s). His views, sometimes unorthodox but always pertinent, are based on wide experience in his famous garden at Great Dixter in East Sussex which is open to the public throughout the summer. The book ranges widely, covering a great variety of plants and skipping nimbly from one subject to another; it is also full of practical suggestions. The author is unusually skilled in combining plants for contrast of flower or foliage, so that each enhances the other, and to prolong the season. Nor does he expect only one crop from much of the border. He grows plants in a reserve bed, and as one dies down it is replaced by another. A book full of ideas, stimulating and exciting.— *Patrick M. Synge*

A Camera up to Nature

A FEW hours after I first met *Eric Hosking*, I was hanging on to his coat as he leaned out of a Sunderland flying boat to photograph Ailsa Craig—a fit introduction to this tireless enthusiast who literally gave AN EYE FOR A BIRD (Hutchinson, 65s) when photographing a tawny owl in Wales. He started with the advantages of a happy and united home but little else, and has become our best-known bird photographer. In the process of collecting some 150,000 pictures, he has had a most exciting and adventurous life. His autobiography, written in collaboration with Frank W. Lane, contains some hitherto unpublished photographs as well as those, like the 'heraldic' barn owl, which are almost his trademark. It does not omit the hard work and stoic patience that underlie his success and is a personal history of the extraordinary progress of bird-watching from being the hobby of a few to an international cult, with his superb pictures as its icons.

WILD WINGS TO THE NORTHLANDS (Witherby, 30s) is the unpretentious diary of a bird-watching trip made by *S. Bayliss Smith* and his brother from the Camargue in April to well beyond the Arctic circle in June. They saw 40 kinds new to them, photographed some and thoroughly enjoyed it all, including the camping life which brought them so close to nature.

'Snowball's' picture first appeared in 'The Countryman' in Winter 1964. Now *Gordon Burness* has written the story of

THE WHITE BADGER (Harrap, 18s) as seen by one of the boys who first reported a 'polar bear' to him. In spite of hazards Snowball has reached the age of seven as the book ends—quite a feat for so conspicuous a creature within 18 miles of central London.

It seems that OTTERS IN THE HOUSE (Longman, 40s) or anywhere else are irresistible. *Joseph A. Davis*, an American zoo curator, describes candidly and with transatlantic humour his attempts to keep a whole series, of several species, at the domestic level. There are photographs and the author's own competent drawings to enhance the appeal of the text, though I must confess I found the tale of failures rather depressing.

That there are half a million of six kinds of WILD DEER IN BRITAIN (D. & Charles, 50s) is, in general, a matter for congratulation. *Roy A. Harris* and *K. R. Duff*, ambidextrous with pen and camera, have produced a handy account of them, notable for its variety of black-and-white photographs, ranging from one of a roebuck marking his territory by rubbing antlers and facial glands against a bush to another showing a newly born sika fawn being ear-tagged. There is a chapter on management and practical conservation, a rather short bibliography and a useful summary of the two Deer Acts.

The latest of Collins's well-produced field guides is a much needed BUTTERFLIES OF BRITAIN AND EUROPE (42s) and it was certainly worth waiting for. *L. G. Higgins* and *N. D. Riley* contribute the compressed text to 760 coloured illustrations by Brian Hargreaves, nearly all from specimens in Dr Higgins's collection and showing a range of subspecies. There are about 380 kinds in the region covered by the authors, so that Britons in Europe, used to only 60, can indeed spread their wings with the help of this authoritative handbook.

THE HAMLYN GUIDE TO BIRDS OF BRITAIN AND EUROPE (25s), for which I was consultant editor, covers more eastern species than any predecessor. It is packed with coloured illustrations by Arthur Singer: a double spread is devoted to the puzzling immature gulls, another to immature and female buntings. Brief text by *Bertel Bruun* faces the main picture of each of the 516 species, with distribution map alongside, achieving *multum in parvo* for the modern bird-watcher.

BIRDS OF WEST CENTRAL AND WESTERN AFRICA (Longman, 120s) is the penultimate volume of the 'African Handbook of Birds', a colossal task undertaken many years ago by *C. W. Mackworth-Praed* and *C. H. B. Grant*. This

Volume I of Series III covers all non-passerine birds and the larks; the rest will follow in a second volume. The coloured and monochrome illustrations, mostly by Chloe Talbot-Kelly and a great improvement on those in the earlier volumes, enrich this indispensable work for the serious student.

Continuing their reproductions of the lithographs of John Gould, Methuen offer BIRDS OF NEW GUINEA (72s), with text by *A. Rutgers*. About 180 species are portrayed, and for those of us for whom an original Gould is beyond reach this book provides an admirable substitute.

Anthony Smith looks at the phenomena of nature primarily in terms of THE SEASONS, Rhythms of Life: Cycles of Change (Weidenfeld, 65s). This is a fresh and attractive approach. I found the earlier chapters, reminding us of our insignificance in the universe and of mysteries unplumbed, more stimulating than those in which he discusses the familiar problems of migration, hibernation, internal clocks and adaptive colour. But it was courageous to tackle so wide a survey, and the book is packed, almost too tight, with interesting facts and statistics. The photographs vary in quality, and I cannot get used to the gimmick of mixing colour and monochrome on the same page.

To mark European Conservation Year the North Wales Naturalists' Trust have published WELSH WILDLIFE IN TRUST (Llys Gwynedd, Bangor, 25s, paperback 18s), a collection of essays and articles, edited by *W. S. Lacey*, on wild life conservation in the widest sense, from the reclamation of the Lower Swansea Valley to the fascinating story of the survival of the kite. All the Welsh trusts and various individuals have co-operated in this review, which concludes with an appendix and map detailing all national parks, nature reserves and other protected areas in Wales.

As an example of the Clue Books published by O.U.P., TREES, by *Gwen Allen* and *Joan Denslow* (15s), strikes me as excellent. There are numerous clear well-captioned colour drawings by Tim Halliday and vignette photographs of each kind *in situ* by Maurice Nimmo. If teachers of rural studies find this book as useful as I think it is, we may yet become a nation of foresters.—*Bruce Campbell*

Ark Endangered

WHEN three out of five new books about animals are concerned with their survival and one with behaviour in captivity, the result is a depressing indictment of man's attitude to wild life. Nevertheless all these books contribute in one way or another to a better understanding of the problems of nature conservation.

WILDLIFE IN DANGER, by *Alan C. Jenkins* (Methuen, 25s), is a short well-balanced introduction to its subject, abundantly and helpfully illustrated. Directed particularly at the younger generation, it deserves to be widely read in schools.

Clive Roots's more detailed WILD HARVEST (Lutterworth, 45s) is not for the squeamish. Much of it is summed up by the title of its opening chapter, 'Commercialised Carnage', but there are occasional lapses from the generally clinical treatment, as in the caption: 'A second away from death, a white-furred seal pup gazes at its executioner with large moist eyes'. The latter part of the book, 'The Sensible Harvest', covers the farming of wild animals, translocation, legitimate hunting and—as befits a curator—the place of zoos.

Few are now unaware of the treasure house of wild life that Africa still is—in parts. Particularly welcome therefore is THE EBONY ARK, by *Eric Robins* (Barrie, 35s), which sets out straightforwardly what various African regimes are doing in conservation. This is another book for the school library; the story of Hugo the hippo and the account of the tiny Abuko nature reserve in the Gambia each has its own quite different lesson.

Not everyone approves of circuses, but even those who do not will find much to fascinate in *Hermann Dembeck's* WILLINGLY TO SCHOOL (Harrap, 35s), most readably translated by Charles Johnson. It tells how apes, elephants, cats of all sizes, dogs, horses and dolphins have been taught a variety of tricks. 'The basis of a successful training method involves complete trust and understanding between man and beast, aided by the animal's play instinct and man's ability to channel that instinct by empathy and scientific knowledge.' Lively anecdote and well-chosen pictures are combined, and the author has a sense of humour. 'Carved monkeys (see no evil, speak no evil, hear no evil) are commonly found on the desks of senior civil servants. Baboons in particular became the patrons of civil servants (because) they are so adaptable.'

For me the pick of this quarter's Ark is undoubtedly *A. M. Harthoorn's* THE FLYING SYRINGE (Bles, 70s), the personal story of a scientist who has done perhaps more than any other to develop the drugs and immobilising techniques now so widely used in the study, rescue and transfer of animals. A good solid book by modern standards, it is notable for its clarity and sustained interest, and also for its humane and balanced approach.

Frankly I do not know what to say about ASKANIA-NOVA, by *L. Heiss* (Bodley, 40s). Notwithstanding its sub-title, 'Animal Paradise in Russia', the book touches on animals only peripherally: it would more accurately be described as an adventurous reconstruction of the lives and fortunes of the Fein and Falz-Fein families between 1763 and 1920. Not until the last 25 pages does one hear at all of the unique menagerie of free-living animals which Friederich Fein created on the Ukraine steppe. Here, in 1914, herds of ante-lopes, eland, zebras, zebroids, llamas, gnus, gazelles, ostriches, buffalo, bison, camels and guanacos were roaming, watched over by mounted shepherds. Twice thereafter Askanian-Nova was devastated by war, to be reconstituted each time as a government research institute, zoo and botanic garden. A full and factual account of this re-markable project from its be-ginnings is still awaited.—*Joe Eggeling*

The Defaulter

IN the private office of a mill in a remote valley near Huddersfield I noticed an old-fashioned clocking-in machine. I asked if it was in honourable retirement. On the contrary, I was assured, it had never been used. It was the first to be installed in the area and the workers ignored it. A special injunction from the proprietor to all departments had no better result. He sent for old Matthew and asked why he had not clocked in and out as instructed.

'Well, tha knaws, Boss, it tak's yoong prentice lads ti larn new tricks an' Ah'm a bit passt that. What's t' idea onyway?'

'I want to find out who comes late.'

'That's easy; there's nobbut thee, so tha might as well put it here in t' private office.'

The boss took Matthew's hint, and there the clock remains.—*George Hudson*

Yellowhammer in snow, by Stephen Dalton

Two cold-weather visitors to Cornish shores: purple sandpiper on rock and grey plover on mud

In winter plumage: Slavonian grebe and black-necked grebe with distinctive uptilted bill.
Photographs by J. B. and S. Bottomley

AS ONE COUNTRYMAN TO ANOTHER

Let him who will believe, and let him who will disbelieve—*Koran*. The worth of men consists in their liability to persuasion—*Whitehead*. The difference is not enough to keep you apart—*William the Silent*. Our business is to speak—*Cromwell*

'THE most important resource is people': these words from the address of Professor J. W. House to the recent Harrogate conference on 'The Changing Uplands' contain the nub of the matter in the north Pennines. Whether their future use is for sheep farming, forestry or recreation, or a combination of the three, people will be required to manage the land. The most intrepid hill-walker surveys a scene that is in part manmade. Sheep will have grazed there or, probably to his dismay, the natural cover will have been replaced with trees. Without man much of the uplands would become overgrown wilderness, offering solitude and little else. They are a reservoir of breeding stock, contributing to the vigour of lowland flocks and providing store lambs and cattle for fattening. For a variety of reasons they are especially attractive to the commercial forester at this time. Yet people are leaving the hills and dales—in a trickle rather than a stream, for the numbers have never been great. The future of many Pennine communities now hangs on the decisions of two or three families—decisions that will almost certainly go unnoticed elsewhere until too late. The Chairman of the North Pennine Rural Development Board, who with the Country Landowners' Association called the conference, was not overstating the case when he referred to 'the threatened collapse of the social fabric' in these hills. They have been suffering from a kind of creeping paralysis; now, especially

Pennine Prospect

FEMALE BRAMBLING WINTERING IN ENGLAND
by Stephen Dalton

O

in the daleheads, they are reaching the point of abrupt collapse. The difficulties of this and other upland areas are repeated in many parts of lowland Britain—declining employment on farms, low remuneration, lack of choice of jobs and career prospects, vanishing public transport—but none is more vulnerable to quite small changes or less able to take advantage of the 'counter tide' which it is the aim of rural policy to encourage. Such studies as have been made confirm that the most important reason for the depopulation of the uplands is the widening of the gap between the real incomes of families there and elsewhere. Many of the older people and some of their children still find a strong sense of community, combined with space and freedom, more enticing than the superficial attractions of the impersonal town. But it is idle to imagine that this will suffice to prevent the disintegration of a fabric already threadbare.

THERE are, of course, significant differences between our upland areas themselves. They vary in climate, landscape, cultural background, proximity to large urban populations, and so in their social and economic problems and opportunities. No one solution will meet all their needs, nor the needs of all. The first requirement is a careful study of each part of each area by a team professionally qualified to evaluate the land from at least half a dozen points of view: agriculture and forestry, small-scale industry, social structure, landscape, conservation of wild life and recreation. The pattern for such a study was worked out in the mid 1960s in east Hampshire. It is now being tested again, in co-operation with some of the principal land users, in the Sherwood Forest. In neither place were industry and the social structure included, as they should be in any future upland study. Its purpose would be to go beyond planning in the customary sense to consider management; and because this is more positive and far-reaching, the objectives would have to be worked out in agreement with all who are likely to be directly affected by subsequent action to achieve them.

CLEAR-CUT management objectives are of the first importance. They are needed to determine how and to what extent farming, forestry, recreation and other uses can best be combined to provide a livelihood for people enough to form socially self-sustaining communites. Farming, and particularly sheep farming, is likely to continue as the mainstay, and the area of forest will certainly grow. Some means must be found, through the price mechanism or production grants, to make sheep farming more worth while. As increasing numbers of people seek space for recreation and lowland farming is intensified, more and more eyes look to the hills. These, too, are becoming more accessible as the motorways are extended: in 1973 a family living in Birmingham will be able to choose between the Lake District and Dartmoor for a day's outing. The freedom of the hills is not something we, individually or as a nation, expect to pay for. But someone has to tend them if they are to remain in the state in which we can enjoy them; and it is right that we should pay for our recreation in so far as it depends on the labours, and may be to the detriment, of others. How can this best be arranged? Sometimes we could pay as we go, but more often than not the collection of small sums of money would be impracticable, especially on unfenced land. The alternative is payment through the well-established channels of public finance. Already farm subsidies contribute indirectly to the control of vegetation and maintenance of traditional landscapes. Once the management objectives are clear, there is much to be said for relating Exchequer payments directly to them. This autumn, after lengthy discussions with representatives of local authorities and owners and occupiers of land, the Countryside Commission published a model access agreement which provides for annual payments in return for the use of land as open space by the public. The payments would include an element of compensation for damage likely to be done, but primarily they would be in the nature of a consideration for this use of the land, which might give rise to constraints on its existing use. With some adaptation this type of agreement could also provide a means to supplement farm incomes in parts of the uplands where public access is not required.

A REGULAR ORDER . . .

with us or with your newsagent is the best way to ensure that you receive future issues of THE COUNTRYMAN. Simply complete the form below, return it to us and we will make all the necessary arrangements. Yearly subscription: Inland 30s, Overseas $5.00 or equivalent in your currency, post paid anywhere in the world. Please send THE COUNTRYMAN to me for a year

MY NAME...

ADDRESS ....

....

I enclose remittance for £............................ $............................

Please arrange for my newsagent to deliver THE COUNTRYMAN to me each quarter at the above address and charge to my account.

NEWSAGENT'S NAME...

ADDRESS ....

....

Signed..4/70

THE COUNTRYMAN, WATLING ST., BLETCHLEY, BUCKS.   **Tel. Bletchley (09-082) 4921**

Countryman Club

If I have sayed amisse I am content that any man amende it, or if I have sayed too little any man that wyll to adde what hym pleaseth to it—*Roger Ascham*

*B*ARMBRACK. My Irish grandmother used to send the raw materials to her bakery across the road. They came back as a great shiny cartwheel bulging with raisins and smelling of spice. We ate the thick slices plastered with butter and wished it could be got in England, till I discovered that it is easy to make; in fact it is the easiest of all yeast mixtures. Here is the recipe. Sift 1 lb. flour and 1 level teasp. mixed spice into a bowl and warm it in a very low oven for a few minutes. Warm 2 oz butter in ½ pint milk gently till melted. Cream ¼ oz yeast with 1 teasp. sugar and add about a third of the lukewarm butter and milk. Make a well in the centre of the flour, pour in the liquid and sprinkle a little flour over it. Cover the bowl with a large plate, fold a towel over it and put it down near the fire to sponge for 20 to 30 minutes. When you take it up, stir in 4 oz each of sultanas and large raisins, 2 oz chopped candied peel, 2 oz sugar, the remaining liquid (warmed again slightly) and a large beaten egg, after setting aside a little of the white for glazing. Mix well. If the dough is too sloppy, sprinkle more flour in it. Knead it well for 15 minutes, first pushing it away

from you, then drawing it towards you, to get the yeast evenly distributed. Then cover the bowl again and put it down by the fire to rise for at least 2½ hours till doubled in bulk. Turn the bowl occasionally so that it is evenly warmed. Knead it again lightly for 5 minutes to knock out air-holes, then put it into a slightly warmed greased 8-in. round tin, cover and set it down to 'prove' for 15 minutes. Bake for 20 minutes at 450° (Regulo 8), then at 400° (Regulo 6) for another 15 minutes. Five minutes before time is up, brush the top with egg-white, sprinkle with castor sugar and return to the oven to finish. Barmbrack is the best and the most satisfying of all tea-breads and will keep fresh for a fortnight, given the chance.— *Maura Clune, Westmorland*

FARMER'S BOY (Summer 1970, p. 263). A ratio of about 20:1 between earnings of 1970 and of 1900 is suggested in the opening sentence. I have it on excellent authority that £1 in 1900 corresponds to about £8 in 1970, so the factor is about 2½ in this context. John Burnett's Pelican, 'A History of the Cost of Living' (1969), shows how the value of money has varied over the last 700 years.—*J. B. Sykes, Berks*

'GHOST' TENNIS COURT (Spring 1970, p. 183). The moving of the lines of daisies is almost eerie, but a probable explanation is the apparent difference in the level of the court and that of the adjoining field. The rainwater, continually draining in one direction, would gradually carry the lime deposits and the daisy growth with it over the years.—*M. Fowler, Warwickshire*

CONNOISSEURS (Autumn 1970, p. 188). For 'phlaridgin' read 'phloridzin'. This is a bitter-tasting crystalline glucoside found primarily in the root bark of fruit trees. It was once used in malaria prevention.—*D. Macer Wright, Glos*

BLACK SPELL BROOK (Summer 1970, p. 328). Folk etymology is almost always erroneous. All 'Spel(l)' placenames signify hundred meetingplaces, from O. E. 'spell' meaning speech or discourse. Spellbrook, a village in Hertfordshire, means 'the meetingplace for speeches beside the brook'. 'Black' in place-names may derive from either of two O. E. adjectives; one means 'bleak, bare of vegetation' or sometimes, of water, 'white with foam', and the other 'black, dark'. I would interpret the name 'Black Spell Brook' as 'the meeting-place for discussions near the black (forest-covered) brook'. It had nothing to do with miners' bad habits, or with tea-making, or with witches and their black spells.—*Douglas Hamer, Sheffield.* [R. J. Jennings comments: 'This is interesting. The brook rises on the edge of a forest path where four ancient rides meet, on the brow of a ridge where for a chain or so the path flattens out. It might well have been a spot chosen for meetings between forest dwellers and officials from very early times, and later for freeminers to meet the gaveller to discuss boundaries or rights to win coal'.]

MINI-TROUSERS. My Wiltshire great-grandmother, seeing her young grandson wearing very short pants, commented: 'Why, they be neither breeches nor trousers nor galleys nor rousers'. In the Vale of Pewsey trousers were sometimes called 'gallirousers', perhaps an example of rhyming slang or an adaptation of 'galligaskins' (loose breeches or gaiters).—*A. E. Davis, Nottingham*

'OLLERTON' CARVINGS (Summer 1970, p. 393). There are several inaccuracies in John Barton's note. My address is Toft, not Ollerton, and I teach sculpture at the Manchester Polytechnic, not

at the University. The correct story of the carvings is as follows. In 1947 the Preston Education Authority kindly allowed me the use of a derelict building, Ribbleton Hall, in the grounds of which the beech tree had grown. It was cut down to make way for a building site and I used the timber for a group of sculptured figures in two parts, depicting War and Peace. The base, which symbolises War, shows a crocodile devouring two fighting figures, victor and vanquished: the vertical part, which fits on top, represents Peace in the form of two figures holding a child, with a lamb and doves. It was six months' work, and when I moved to Toft I took it with me, but brought it indoors after some years because of deterioration by weathering. The local authority did not ask me to remove it, though it did attract a great deal of attention and visitors called at all hours, even in the middle of the night.— *Edward Roocroft, Cheshire*

Answers to Correspondents

We feed on questions—*Athenaeus*. Not every question deserves an answer—*P. Syrus*

DONKEY BITES. I was feeding my friendly jenny donkey with a titbit when, to my pain, she took a good mouthful of fingers and hung on hard. What went wrong?— *B. M. C., Oxon.* [Marjorie Dunkels, in 'Training Your Donkey' (J. A. Allen, 10s 6d), has this to say: 'Presenting a hand flat with the thumb stuck well out to the side is asking for trouble. Make a cup of your hand with the thumb tucked and shaped into the cup, and offer the present directly under the nose. The hurt expression on the donk's face, when an extended thumb turns out not to be a carrot, is almost as disturbing as the hurt expression of the person whose thumb it was. Very small children should be discouraged from offering presents at all'.—*Editor*]

RIGHTS OF WAY. We have had several inquiries about the duties and rights of footpath users. Particularly local problems are best referred to the nearest Field Paths Society or branch of the Ramblers' Association. A good general guide is 'Law of Footpaths', published at 4s by the Commons, Open Spaces and Footpaths Preservation Society. For the pocket there is a sixpenny leaflet, 'Right of Way', issued by the Ramblers' Association. See our 'Directory of Useful Addresses' on p. 413.—*Editor*

BLUE GULLS. Can you explain an optical illusion? About 3 o'clock· on a lovely autumn afternoon, with the sun about 20° above the horizon and immediately behind me, I came to Johnson's Pond by Virginia Water, a small sheet so closely surrounded by trees that the water and the air for some feet above it were in deep shadow. Floating on the pond was a bright blue gull. I am not colour-blind; having been for many years in the fashion end of the textile trade, I am rather good at colours. Besides, my daughters saw it blue too: not the sort of blue an artist sees in a shadow, but a real sky blue. Presently the bird rose and the blue of its wings was startling; but as it flew into the sunshine the blue disappeared and it reverted to an ordinary grey and white gull. When it dipped into the shadow again, the blue reappeared. My daughters, who had walked to the other side of the pond, facing the sun, said that the blue was not apparent to them.—*J. H. B. Gowan, Bucks.* [Shortly after receiving this letter, I saw 'blue' black-headed gulls under similar conditions on Blenheim Lake. A physicist whom I consulted pointed out that the light which illuminates an object in shadow is diffuse or scattered, and therefore predominantly blue. This preferential scattering of blue light is known as the Rayleigh Effect. I believe that the blue look is not more often recorded because bird-watchers know that gulls are supposed to be grey and white and refuse to see them in any other colour.—*B. C.*]

'*GRANFER-GRIGGLES*'. A friend gave this name to a beautifully marked flower, probably an orchid, which she used to see in the North Dorset countryside. What is its correct name?—*Vera Hickson, Dorset.* [Wright's 'English Dialect Dictionary' gives 'granfergiggles' and 'granfer-goslings' for *Orchis mascula*, 'granfergregors' for wild hyacinth, and 'granfer-griggles' for either of these or for red campion. 'Gosling' was a term for things in season when young goslings hatch: a 'gosling blast' might herald an April shower.—*A. F.*]

REPAIRS TO RUSH CHAIRS (*M. C. B.*). Reseating of rush chairs can often be arranged through a county Association for the Blind. Restorations and repairs are also undertaken by E. M. F. Brown (Quality Town) Ltd, Church Lane, West Wycombe, High Wycombe, Bucks; rushing is one of their specialities.—*Editor*

394

Sign of Gratitude

There are many lonely and anxious old people for whom eth Methodist Homes for the Aged are a haven and a home. Will you please join the growing number of people, grateful for their own security and peace-of-mind who remember the Methodist Homes for the Aged in their Will? Even with 28 Homes for the Aged we can accommodate only a few of the many hundreds on our waiting list. Please write to the General Secretary, Rev. R. J. Connell, BA, BD for brochure "A Gift for Caring" and suggested form of words for a Will or Codicil—or consult your Solicitor, Accountant or Bank Manager.

Methodist Homes for the Aged

1 Central Buildings,
Westminster, London, S.W.1

FARM WAGGONS OF ENGLAND & WALES
by James Arnold

A limited signed edition: a unique book. 24 full colour illustrations and long text. Folio size, 130s (only a few)

SEA FISHING FOR BEGINNERS
by Maurice Wiggin

A painless guide to piscatorial pleasure. All you need to know to go fishing from shore, pier, jetty, rocks and boats. Line drawings. 21s

5 Royal Opera Arcade
Pall Mall, London SW1
or from any bookshop

The Thoroughbred

PETER WILLETT

This beautifully illustrated book traces the evolution of the breed, and, for the first time, examines the development—from British stock—of thoroughbred breeding in the major racing countries. The superb illustrations, which include 32 pages in colour, consist of paintings, engravings, prints, caricatures and photographs.

85s.

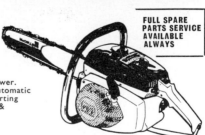

PICTUREMARKET

of CRAFT PRODUCTS for home and garden

No. 17 Ducks Rising

Aluminium Weather Vanes and Garden Furniture

Exclusive items our speciality
Please write for brochure to:

Norbank Products

BLO'NORTON, DISS, NORFOLK
Telephone Botesdale 242

PORCHES

DOORS

TABLES

WINDOWS

STAIRCASES

C. F. PUTTERILL LTD.
HARPENDEN HERTS. Tel: 4626-8
We exhibit at the London and
Cambridge Building Centres.

A true 'hand' craft! A wide range of rush-woven products including Log Baskets, Carpets and Mats, etc.

Send for illustrated brochure.

W.A.G. LTD., Aldeby, Beccles, Suffolk. Tel.: Aldeby 345/6/7/8

Now is the time to Plan your Spring layout to include a Regency Pool. You can afford one, prices range from £250, to the largest at approx. £600, all in durable ever-lasting fibreglass. Pool owners—send for our leaflet on 'Pool Care' etc.
REGENCY SWIMMING POOLS, Compton Road, Wolverhampton. Telephone Wolverhampton 27709.

FOR BIRD LOVERS

THE RIKDEN

BIRDBATH

Handmade, 20″ diameter, tough, light fibre-glass, good clawgrip. Will not crack in frost nor be damaged by boiling water. Lasts for years. Holds 1½ gals. and 8 or 9 birds. On feet, will not harbour slugs nor harm grass. **State colour required: Copper Green or Dark Grey. Price £2 plus postage and packing 9/6d.**
R. Dendy (C4), 2 Aultone Yard,
Aultone Way, Carshalton, Surrey.

Original Designs, in Silver and Gold, based on Norse Mythology and Shetland Antiquities.

Send for Free Brochure.
SHETLAND SILVER-CRAFT, Weisdale, Shetland.

SMALLS

Rates:—'Personal' 2s 6d per word, prepaid, minimum 30s. Heavy type advertisements in border (1⅜in. by 3⅜in.) £8 8s 0d per insertion, prepaid. Other categories 2s per word, prepaid, minimum 24s. Heavy type in border £7 7s 0d per insertion, prepaid. Box No. (which counts as two words) 2/- extra. Cuttings on request. Advertisements should reach us not later than mid-January for insertion in the Spring 1971 Number, published early March, and should be addressed to the Classified Advertisement Manager, The Countryman, 23-27 Tudor Street, London, E.C.4 (Tel.: 01-583 9199, Ex. 307)

PERSONAL

Audrey Allen Country Marriage Bureau, Poughill, Bude, Cornwall. Est. 1955. Member British Marriage Bureaux Association. Nationwide, confidential service. Details sent under plain sealed cover without obligation

Animal Lovers. Oil paintings from photographs of horses, dogs, etc. Likeness guaranteed. Photos of paintings available. Jean Walker, Cannons, Tibberton (309), Glos., GL19 3AB

Antique, Carriage, Grandfather and Bracket Clocks, bought, sold and restored. T. R. Nelson, 177 The Crescent, Walsall, Staffs. Walsall 28819

As a Christmas Gift (7/6d posted direct)—Little Books of the Open Air. No. 1—Countryside Secrets (Geoffrey Eley), No. 2—Pleasure Angle, recollections of a thoughtful fisherman (W. A. Stevens). Or, at 16/6d post free, the Duke of Edinburgh award-winning Two Ears of Barley (J. C. Wilkerson), Priory Press, Royston (Herts.). Tel.: 42313

The Ashley Marriage Bureau, 10 Corporation Street, Manchester 4 (Est. 1953). Our personal service covers all parts of the country. Special Professional and Executive Register. Ideal for those interested in cultural activities and country life

Authors Invited Submit MSS all types (including Poems) for book publication. Reasonable terms. Stockwell Ltd., Ilfracombe. (Est. 1898)

Better Than Shares. Breed Shetlands. Booklet entitled 'Shetland and You' 6/-. Morgan-Davies, Wellington, Somerset

Calendar of the Countryside for 1971, Wildlife Notelets, Christmas Cards, Toys, Books. Send for Brochure, Christian Action (CM), 105 Newgate Street, London, E.C.1.

Christmas Cards that are Different! Original wood engravings, colour prints, etc. from The Cocklands Press, Burford, Oxford. Retail prices from 4d. 50% Trade discount. Samples post free in the U.K. General printing also undertaken

Friendship/Marriage Centre. Confidential. Nationwide. Details Dept. RY, 33 Sheringham Avenue, London, N.14

Friendship Marriage. Members all ages, everywhere! Confidential. Details s.a.e. World Friendship Enterprises, CX74, Amhurst Park, London, N.16

PERSONAL—*continued*

Galt Toys have been in daily use for years in kindergartens, playgroups and homes of all thinking parents. Shopping-by-post catalogue free. Galt Toyshops: 30/31 Gt. Marlborough Street, London, W.1; 60 Princes Street, Edinburgh; 25 Bridge Street Row, Chester; Cheadle, Cheshire

Hard Skin? Corns? Do Try Pickles Ointment. It's good. Ask your Chemist or send 3/6d. Pickles House, Church Lane, Knaresborough, Yorkshire

Industrial Archaeology, our lively quarterly, grows in size and stature. 50/- per annum. David & Charles, Newton Abbot

Lifelong Present. Your daughter's wedding professionally recorded on an unbreakable LP. Safely despatched anywhere. Sound News, 18 Blenheim Road, W.4. 01-995 1661

ENGLISH SCHOOLS . . . For free advice, based on nearly a century of experience, about BOARDING and FINISHING SCHOOLS, SECRETARIAL COLLEGES and TUTORS, consult: **THE GABBITAS-THRING EDUCATIONAL TRUST, 6/8 Sackville Street, LONDON, W1X 2BR (01-734 0161)**

'Lloyds Euxesis'—Still the Finest Brushless Shave—Even After 160 Years. Send 30/- for 6 tubes direct from Aimee Lloyd & Co., Ltd., Tenterden, Kent

Maritime History. This is a new half-yearly journal which sees publication in April 1971 and will contain illustrated articles based on current research, with emphasis on international merchant shipping, ports, naval architecture, maritime law and insurance. Annual subscription £1.50, single copies 90p. David & Charles, Newton Abbot

Marjorie Moore's Marriage Bureau. Introductions Confidentially Arranged. Free Details from Dept. C., 79 New Bond Street, London, W.1

---

4 CLASSIC BOOKS ON CRAFTS

'Folk-Cross-Stitch-Design' by Heinz Edgar Kiewe, £3.17.6. U.S.A. and Canada postage free $9.99. **'History of Folk-Cross-Stitch'** by Heinz Edgar Kiewe, £1.12.6. Linen-bound, Post-paid to U.S.A. and Canada, $3.80. **'Africa: Make Them Craftsmen'** by Heinz Edgar Kiewe (with Michael Biddulph), £1.8.6. Post-paid to U.S.A. and Canada $4.00. **'The Sacred History of Knitting'** by Heinz Edgar Kiewe, £1.14.6. Fully illustrated volume, 2nd edition, $4.99. **A.N.I. ART NEEDLEWORK INDUSTRIES LTD., Ship Street, Oxford, England**

Not Hearing Too Well? Maybe the cause is wax that has accumulated. Remove the cause with gentle Earex. From all chemists

Oil Painting of your favourite photograph by Hazel Folkes, Blackwood House Cottage, Horton, near Leek, Staffs.

HEATHER JENNER MARRIAGE BUREAU, 124 New Bond Street, W.1. 01-629 9634. SCOTLAND, EDINBURGH, 031-667 5527. **WEST COUNTRY, BRISTOL,** OBR2 684421. **LANCASHIRE,** 0391-5 24005. **BIRMINGHAM, HEREFORD** 5276. **KENT, HAM STREET,** 255. **EAST ANGLIA,** 06053 2879. **JEWISH BRANCH,** 01-452 6086

The School They Talk About On The Radio. In four broadcasts the work of the LSJ has been praised by successful students who have been interviewed. The standard of personal coaching by correspondence is unsurpassed. Get the Jubilee issue of Writing for the Press from: The London School of Journalism (C.M.), 19 Hertford Street, Park Lane, London, W1Y 8BB. Tel.: 01-499 8250

Shirts to Measure. Write for wide choice of patterns from A. C. Garstang Ltd., 213 Preston New Road, Blackburn

---

ARE YOU SATISFIED WITH YOUR NOTEPAPER?

If you like 'The Countryman' you will probably like us since we belong to the same Group.

Pulmans have been printers since 1787, and according to Company legend we printed letterheadings for both the Duke of Wellington and for Napoleon.

We print quality, and as such serve about a dozen embassies, members of the Royal Family, and several thousand professional people.

If you care to write we will send you samples of styles and papers for both Letter-press (general use) and Diestamping (special use) with prices.

On receipt of your order, delivery is about 2-3 weeks.

GEORGE PULMAN STATIONERS LIMITED
24/27 Thayer Street, London, W.1
Phone: 01-935 8261

Strong Well Designed Wooden Toys for a lifetime's play available direct from manufacturer. Write for illustrated list: Poyle, Bainton, Stamford, Lincs.

Wulcosa Collar Attached Shirts sizes 14½"-18½" in stock. Patterns on request stating size. Thos. H. Barford Ltd., Uckfield, Sussex. Established over 70 years

ANCESTRAL RESEARCH

Ancestors Traced. Pedigrees compiled. All forms of historical and ancestral research undertaken, Deeny & Sword, Genealogists, 12 Duke Street, London, S.W.1. Whitehall 6988. Consultations by appointment

ANTIQUES, BOOKS, MAPS AND PICTURES

Aesthetic but not Rolling? For good antiques still at reasonable prices write for Catalogue to Margery Dean, B.A., Antiques, Wivenhoe, Essex

Antiquarian, Secondhand and Rare Books on the Countryside, Natural History, Ornithology, Animal Behaviour, Fishing and Sailing and Rural Sports. Postal Service, Handsome catalogue free. Bright Hill Books, Great Rollright, Oxon.

Books on Windmills, Dowsing, Railways, Birds, Sundials, Ferns, Heraldry, Names, Antiquities, Bells, King Penguins, rare Topography, Art, Music, Literature, Travel, and many other subjects. Current catalogue contains 2,000 out-of-print items. 5/- post free. Refundable. Serendip Books, Lyme Regis, Dorset

'The Countryman' 1951 to 1969 unbound. Offers Coltman, 14 Wheatlands Road, Harrogate

'The Countryman,' Spring 1942 to Winter 1946, and Spring 1948 to Winter 1968, plus nine odd copies from 1931. Total 113 copies. Offers? Doncaster, 19 Fifehead Magdalen, Gillingham, Dorset

Every Book on Farming, Gardening and Forestry available for sale by post. Secondhand titles stocked. Experienced advice free. Catalogue 1/6d (refundable on 20/- purchase), Landsman's Bookshop, Buckenhill, Bromyard, Hereford

Interesting Second-Hand Books. Natural History, Gardening, Countryside, General. List from Littlewood, 160 Staincliffe Road, Dewsbury, Yorkshire

---

COUNTRY BOOKS ARE OUR SPECIALITY
Suggested new titles for Winter reading and giving are: **The Natural History of the Lake District** 60s. **The Batsford Book of Dogs** 30s. **A History of Farm Buildings in England and Wales** 60s. **Owls**, their natural and unnatural history 50s. **Wild Deer in Britain**, an illustrated study, 50s. **Farm Animals in Colour**, 158 breeds described and illustrated 25s. **Rural Costume**, its origin and development in Western Europe and the British Isles, 378 line illustrations, 80s. All these books **AVAILABLE POST FREE FROM H. LOWE & CO., COUNTRY BOOKS, 18 Town Street, THAXTED, DUNMOW, ESSEX**

CLOTHING

Almost 'Unwearoutable' Socks and Stockings knit in wool/nylon mixture. Many of these have been worn for six months or more in Wellingtons with never a hole. For shades and samples write Nichol, Knitter, Corbridge, Northumberland

---

ARAN HAND-KNIT SWEATERS of quality and distinction in traditional oiled wool. A MUST for every countryman's wardrobe and an asset for every fashion conscious lady Write for illustrated brochure 2/- **—JESSIE BARKER, 115 High Street, Bangor, N. Ireland**

Country Skirts Tailored to Measure from our famous Scottish Tweeds. Style brochure and patterns. Tweeds also sold by the yard. D. & M. Grant, Killin, Perthshire

Donegal Hand-woven Tweeds. Hand-knitted sweaters, cardigans, Aran patterns. Patterns sent. Mrs. Baker, Portsalon, Letterkenny, Donegal, Eire

Handwoven Donegal Tweed Skirts to measure and Tweed Lengths, also Matching Knitwear and Handknitted 'Arans'. Write for Patterns to Mary Howard-Johnson, 28 Bodnant Avenue, Leicester

---

W. BILL LTD., SPECIALISTS IN FINE TWEEDS and knitwear since 1846. Our famous shop at 93 New Bond Street contains a wealth of hand-loomed Shetland and Harris tweeds and a wide range of Shetland, cashmere, lambswool and alpaca knitwear for ladies and men. Make a personal visit, or write for our catalogue. **W. BILL LTD., 93 New Bond Street, London, W.1**

406

CLOTHING—*continued*

Hand-woven Harris Tweeds, traditional and new designs, samples free. Also Scotch tweeds, suitings, tartans, Aran, Shetland, cashmere and lambswool sweaters. Suit and kilt making service. Samples free. Refund guarantee. MacGillivray & Company, Muir of Aird, Benbecula, Scotland

Knitting Wools. Aran 1/5d-1/7d oz. Shetland 2/6d-2/9d oz. S.A.E. samples. Achins Weavers and Knitters, Lochinver, West Sutherland

Knitwear, Cashmere and Lambswool, by Pringle of Scotland, 'Braemar' and other specialists. Brochures available from Watt of Brechin, 14-18 Swan Street, Brechin, Angus

---
HUSKY OF TOSTOCK LTD, 115 BURY ST, STOWMARKET, SUFFOLK
Manufacturers of thermo insulated clothing for all sporting and outdoor people. Car Coats & Casuals. Fishing Coats & Tweed Shooting Coats. Executive Range of all purpose 100% waterproofs. Insulated underwear & sox. Send for **FREE BROCHURE**

Ladies' All Wool or Lisle Stockings, all fully fashioned. Details Musgroves (C), Kendal, Westmorland

Slacks, Skirts, Made-to-Measure from 63/-. Ladies', Gent's, Children's. Also Jodhpurs, Jackets, Shooting Knickers. Write now for measurement form and patterns stating your requirements. We have all types of cloths and make to any style. Hebden Cord Co., Ltd. (Dept. CM), Hebden Bridge, Yorkshire

Tweeds for Shooting, Country and Business Wear are our speciality. Also our far famed Ladies' Costume Tweeds. Patterns sent on request. P. & J. Haggart Ltd., Woollen Manufacturers, Aberfeldy, Perthshire

---
NO MORE DARNING! Socks for Heavy Boots. Guaranteed 10 months. Letters seen by 'The Countryman' proving 7 years' wear without holes! Lovat, Bronze, Navy, Grey. For Boots 7-13. 3 pairs 24/-. State Boot Size. Stockings available.
TRENN SUPPLY COMPANY (C34), P.O. Box 5, Long Eaton, Nottingham

---

DOGS AND CATS, ETC.

Animal Portraits from Photographs, charcoal, oils, water-colour. Will draw from life, if owner lives in Sussex. Anne Williams, 10a Hollington Park, St. Leonards-on-Sea, Sussex. Hastings 3987

Cat Lovers. Give your pet a wonderful Christmas present—a 'Walcott Pussflap'. Draughtproof, beautifully made, easy to fit, giving freedom to your cat. 35/6d including postage. Walcott Petware, Hawling, Andoversford, Glos. Leaflet available

---
THE ACME *SILENT* **DOG WHISTLE**
Renowned for its inaudibility and receptiveness to all dogs. 17/6d each, including Tax and Postage. From all dealers, otherwise contact the manufacturers:
J. HUDSON & CO. (WHISTLES) LTD., BARR STREET, BIRMINGHAM, 19

FARM AND GARDEN

Beekeeping Appliances. Catalogue, 4d stamp. Burtt & Son, Stroud Road, Gloucester

Extension Ladders and Steps, of all types and sizes in wood and aluminium for home, garden and farm. Disappearing Loft Ladders. Catalogues free from manufacturers, Drew, Clark & Co., Ltd., 'Diamond' Ladder Works, Leyton, London, E.10

Plant Tubs. Water Butts. Dovecotes. Hazel/Willow Hurdles. Teak/Rustic Furniture. Brochure. Battersbys (C), Norfolk Way, Uckfield, Sussex

Uncommon Vegetable Seed and Herb Catalogue. Lavender and Pot-Pourri Sachets 3/6d each post free. Also Herbal Remedy Catalogue. Write to Miss Kathleen Hunter, Argyll Herbal Remedies, Barcaldine House, Connel, Argyll

---
WILDBIRD FOOD 5lb 9/9, 13lb 17/-, 28lb 24/6, 56lb 42/-, cwt 82/-. **RAISINS** 5lb 13/-, 13lb 27/3, 28lb 48/9, 56lb 89/-, cwt 174/-. **PEANUTS** (kernels) 5lb 13/-, 13lb 25/6, 28lb 43/9, 56lb 82/-, cwt 160/-. Carr. paid. Not for human consumption. List from **JOHN E. HAITH LTD., Dept. C, PARK STREET, CLEETHORPES**

FOOD

Abandon Dull Meals. We invite you to write for our unadorned but straightforward Christmas List. We only sell the Best of Foodstuffs accurately described and sincerely praised. Many consist of our own Direct Imports, only obtainable from us in the U.K. Our offers have appeared weekly in the National Press for 35 years, and at present appear each week in 'The Times', 'Country Life' and 'The Observer'. Our Coffee originally sold at 1/- per lb is still the Best and Cheapest. Shilling Coffee Co., Ltd., 29 Mitre Street, London, E.C.3

Black Isle Oatmeal. Dr. Johnson's definition of oats—admittedly made to vex the Scots—was: 'A grain, which in England is generally given to horses, but in Scotland supports the people'. To which the reply was made: 'Yes, Sir, but where will you find such horses and such people?' Hendersons, Dingwall. Samples sent Post Free

Honey for Health. Buy in bulk 60lb Drum Pure Australian Honey £6 15s 0d. Full lists of honeys of the World. N.B.B.H.C., Market Place, Grantham, Lincs.

Wholefood, Compost grown unsprayed flours, cereals, vegetables in season. Send for lists, or try our £1 Tasting Parcel of delicious dried fruits as Christmas presents. Wholefood, 112 Baker Street, London, W.1

GENERAL

Antique Oak and Mahogany Furniture. Lawson Antiques Ltd., Tonbridge. Telephone 2183

A Present from Lincs. Lucky Bootscraper and Boot Jack on Handmade Shepherds Crook. Last a lifetime, c/paid £5 5s 0d. Ideal gift. (Wrought Iron.) J. G. Blakey & Son, Market Rasen, Lincs.

Calling All Cooks. Keep your kitchen knives handy and sharp with a Wall Fitting Teak Knife Rack, holding up to six knives and incorporating a very efficient sharpener. Post paid 25/6d from J. Sturrock, Bryn, Caernarvon, N. Wales

Carved Oak Footstools to mark great anniversaries, Weddings, Birthdays, Retirements. Names, dates inscribed. Individually designed. Five guineas. Pringle, 145 Hillmorton Road, Rugby

Cemcol—the new waterproof paint cures leaking pools, proofs and recolours concrete, asbestos and wooden buildings. Available in 7 colours. 1 gallon covers 280-360 sq. ft. 13/5d pint, 75/- gallon. From Decorators' Merchants. Details from Grangersol Ltd., Imperial Way, Watford, Herts.

Jig-Saw Puzzles on Loan. Details from the Hampstead Jig-Saw Club, 48 Heath Drive, Potters Bar, Hertfordshire

Pipe Smoker? The cost of top quality briar pipes is becoming more and more prohibitive. Write for our free catalogue of a famous London manufacturer's genuine seconds. Smooth, Sandblast, Natural, Straight Grain, etc. From 15/- each. Walbourn Smith and Company, 26 Worthing Road, East Preston, Littlehampton, Sussex.

Reproduction Dining Chairs. Individually hand-made. Thomas Hudson, Half Thatch, Odell, Bedfordshire

Solid Oak Garden Gates, made by Craftsmen. Stamp for details, Fletcher, Joiner, 36 The Green, Haughton-Le-Skerne, Darlington

HOTELS, GUEST HOUSES & HOLIDAY ACCOMMODATION

LONDON. A friendly welcome extended to all visitors at inexpensive Private Hotel. Full Central Heating, Colour TV and other amenities. Morning tea and breakfast, single 32/-, double 30/- each per night, reductions over four nights and children under twelve, youngest child Free, December, January and February. Reserve, or request descriptive Brochure. B. C. Hodgson, *Warrington House Hotel*, 1 *Warrington Crescent, LONDON, W9 1ED*

FARM HOLIDAYS—Get the latest Farm Holiday Guide with Britain's best farm houses covering every county from Land's End to John o'Groats; price 4/- (postage 1/8d). Farm Holiday Guide, Dept. C., 18 High Street, Paisley

A NEW HOTEL IN WILDEST WALES. Central heating throughout, private bathrooms. 1,000 feet a.s.l. 6 miles trout fishing. *Llwynderw Hotel, ABERGWESYN, BRECKNOCK.* Llanwrtyd Wells 238

A SIMPLE HOLIDAY. *MERIONETHSHIRE, N. WALES.* Country quiet, cooking and comfort. 2 to 5 guests. Car necessary. Box No. 303 'The Countryman'

AYNSOME MANOR HOTEL, *CARTMEL, NEAR GRANGE-OVER-SANDS.* Delightful, welcoming house with Adam features in 12th Century Priory Village. Beautiful countryside close Kent and Leven Estuaries and Lakes Windermere and Coniston. Ideal Spring holidays. Signpost recommended. Telephone Cartmel 276

BERKSHIRE. *Charney Manor, Quaker Guest House, CHARNEY BASSETT, NEAR WANTAGE.* Country holidays in thirteenth century manor house, large walled garden. Brochure from the Wardens. Tel.: West Hanney 206

BETWEEN NEW FOREST AND SOLENT Bird Sanctuary. Quiet, 18th century charm, central heating, heated swimming pool, good food, licensed. *Fishers Mead Hotel, KEYHAVEN, LYMINGTON, HANTS.*

CORNWALL. A small highly recommended Hotel, superb walks and coastal scenery in a truly rural setting. Ideal base for touring the North Cornish and Devon coastlines. Good food, personal service and a warm welcome await you at *Trelawny Hotel, WIDEMOUTH BAY, NEAR BUDE, CORNWALL.* Tel.: W.B. 328. AA* RAC*

COTSWOLDS. *The Golden Ball, BURFORD,* a small informal Inn offering personal service to the individual. Pride is taken in the quality and cooking of traditional English food. A Country Holiday is offered in unspoilt and uncrowded conditions without being too remote

DEVON. *West Bradford Country House, BRADFORD, HOLSWORTHY,* offers adult guests every comfort, excellent cuisine (Restaurant licence), real service. Brochure from Miss Crocker

EAST DEVON. Estuary village noted for bird life. Good area for fishing, sailing, golf. Guests welcome pleasant, modernised, quietly situated cottage. 2 *Stepps Orchard, AXMOUTH, EX12 4AR*

S.E. DEVON. Coast 3 miles. Country house midst own peaceful fields and woods offers gracious holiday living from May to October. Brochure. *Lovehayne, SOUTHLEIGH, COLYTON, DEVON*

SOUTH DEVON. *Hinds Hill, EAST PRAWLE, NEAR KINGSBRIDGE.* Phone Chivelstone 263. Standing 400 ft above sea level with panoramic views of rolling coastline and English Channel where ships of many nations regularly pass. Offers quiet but luxurious accommodation. 6 Bedrooms. 3 Bathrooms. Sorry, no children or pets. Brochure upon request

SOUTH DEVON. Country House Hotel with ½ mile trout fishing, within easy reach of beaches, sailing, Dartmoor, riding and golf. Children very welcome. Ashley Courtenay recommended. Licensed. Mr. & Mrs. Douglas Miller, *The Old Mill, HARBERTON, TOTNES.* Harbertonford 349

ENGLISH LAKES. *Grange Hotel, LOWESWATER, COCKERMOUTH.* 17th Century manor house set in own grounds. Beautiful, unspoiled countryside. Good food and wines. Fires, part central heating. Open all the year. Tel.: Lamplugh 211

EXMOOR. Wonderful coastal and inland walking from complete rural seclusion of attractively modernised self-contained wing old Devon farmhouse available for up to four considerate holiday tenants. Box No. 302 'The Countryman'

EXMOOR, *NEAR WOODY BAY.* Best of both worlds, peace of the countryside, easy reach North Devon's Coves, Beaches. Ideal Walkers, Bird-Watchers, Explorers. An attractive Country Guest House in a beautiful setting. 20 acres own Moorland. Brochure, Adams, *Cherryford, MARTINHOE, PARRACOMBE, N. DEVON.* Parracombe 285

EXMOOR. *The Manor House, LUCCOMBE, MINEHEAD.* Private country house in lovely setting offers real comfort, warmth and peace. Also, two self-contained annexes available for holiday letting. Write owners for brochure

EXMOOR. *Outovercott, LYNTON.* Situated in own valley in Exmoor National Park. Horses and ponies for hire. Beaches. Log fires. Brochure with pleasure. Lynton 3341

EXMOOR BORDERS. A charming cottage for self-catering holidays, with peace and tranquillity, to sleep 6. The whole most comfortably furnished by the discerning countryman. Spring and Autumn idyllically suited for walking. Details:—D. A. Adams, *Trentishoe Manor, PARRACOMBE, BARNSTAPLE, N. DEVON.* Parracombe 398

EXMOOR BORDERS. Solitary modern caravan with annexe, sleeps 7, all mains, hot water by immersion, bath, flush w.c. Heavenly valley. Spring and Autumn idyllically suited for walking. Details:—D. A. Adams, *Trentishoe Manor, PARRACOMBE, BARN-STAPLE, N. DEVON.* Parracombe 398

FRIENDLY OLD HOUSE between moors and sea welcomes guests seeking quiet, lovely country, good cooking. *Allerford House, ALLERFORD.* Porlock 592

HAMPSHIRE, *WINCHESTER. Chantry Mead Hotel,* 2767. Small comfortable Hotel. Good food. Helpful service

LAKE DISTRICT. *Bridge Hotel, BUTTERMERE.* Friendly welcome and superb scenery make this an ideal base for Lakeland exploration. 25 bedrooms, two lounges, Bar (conditional licence). Special clothes-drying room. Dogs welcome. A.A**., R.A.C. Write for brochure

LOVELY ROSEDALE. Delightful Residential Hotel. A.A., R.A.C., Egon Ronay, 'Wave' Recommended. Set amid glorious scenery of the North Yorkshire National Park and offering comfort, good food and a warm welcome. Fishing, riding, pony trekking, golf, fell walking, touring. *The Milburn Arms, ROSEDALE ABBEY, PICKERING, YORK-SHIRE.* Tel.: Lastingham 312

MALVERN HILLS. For Winter or Summer walking, fine views and good touring. You will feel welcome at this small hotel with its quiet situation, modest tariff, central heating throughout. Brochure. Mrs. R. Fisher, *Sherington Hotel, Priory Road, MALVERN, WORCS.* Malvern 3266

NORFOLK—THE LINKS HOTEL, WEST RUNTON, CROMER
Open all the year. Sea and country. Fully licensed. Private bathrooms. Nine hole Golf Course adjoins Hotel. Resident Directors: Mr. and Mrs. B. H. Plumpton.
A.A.   **Telephone: West Runton 413**   **R.A.C.**

NORTH ARGYLL. For a quiet holiday in some of Scotland's finest sea and hill scenery relax at *The Kilchoan Hotel.* Comfortable, good food, fully licensed. Syers-Gibson, *Kilchoan Hotel, ARDNAMURCHAN.* Kilchoan 200

NORTH PEMBROKESHIRE. Friendly welcome in mediaeval farmhouse in unchanging Gwaun Valley. Home produced food. Roberts, *Garn, LLANYCHAER, FISHGUARD*

POLRUAN, *CORNWALL.* Waterside cottage, furnished as very comfortable home. Beautiful views, walking, sailing, domestic help. Box No. 306 'The Countryman'

SARK, *CHANNEL ISLANDS*—the unspoilt island for a really restful holiday. *Hotel Petit Champ.* Unrivalled secluded position, magnificent views. Fully licensed to guests; central heating; rooms with private bathrooms. For illustrated brochure write or phone Sark 46. Mr. and Mrs. J. M. Scott

SNOWDONIA NATIONAL PARK, *NEAR DOLGELLAU, MERIONETH.* In private grounds, 3 bedroomed flat sleeps 6. Fully furnished, bathing beaches 10 miles. Delightful walks and scenery. Box No. 305 'The Countryman'

SPRING COMES EARLY IN DEVON. Why not arrive with the lambs and the buds at *Glebe House Hotel, NORTH BOVEY, DEVON?.* P.S. Central heating just in case

TRANQUILLITY in remote, peaceful and friendly *SHETLAND.* Good food, wines, comfort and personal attention from the Resident Proprietors at *Voe Country House Hotel, VOE, SHETLAND.* (Tel.: Voe 241). Ideally centred for Rambling, Sightseeing, Bird-watching and Trouting. Central Heated throughout. Brochure on request

WALKERS' PARADISE: Cottage Guest House, Exmoor National Park. Excellent home cooking. March-October. C.H., H.&C. From 9½ gns. S.A.E. Brochure. *Fern Cottage, ALLERFORD, NEAR MINEHEAD, SOMERSET.* Porlock 215

WELSH BORDER *(HEREFORDSHIRE).* Cottage, lovely country near Black Mountains. Bed, breakfast and evening meal. Box No. 304 'The Countryman'

WEST SUTHERLAND. *Achins, INVERKIRKAIG, LOCHINVER.* Hot and Cold all bedrooms. Great interest to naturalists, peaceful surroundings. Brochure

WILTS./DORSET BORDER. A quiet hotel in the Cranborne Chase where walking is a joy and motoring still a pleasure. Fully licensed. A warm welcome awaits you. *King John's Hotel. TOLLARD ROYAL, WILTSHIRE.* Tollard Royal 207

YORKSHIRE PENNINES. *NIDDERDALE.* A warm welcome by the owners and every comfort awaits you at this charming old Dales Farmhouse. Open all year. Ideal motoring, walking. Wildlife. Beautiful scenery. Good English cooking. H.&C., C.H. all rooms. Comfortable lounges, log fires. S.A.E. Brochure, Bernard and Joy Waddell, *Low Green House, WATH, PATELEY BRIDGE, HARROGATE.* Tel.: Pateley Bridge 322

PROPERTY

Cheltenham and the Cotswolds. For Town and Country Properties, G. H. Bayley & Sons, Chartered Surveyors, Chartered Auctioneers and Estate Agents. Established in Cheltenham for over one hundred years. 27 Promenade, Cheltenham. Tel.: Cheltenham 21102/3/4

WANTED

Antique Carriage Clock, preferably but not necessarily one needing restoration. Box No. 307 'The Countryman'

Copy of Thomas Okey's book 'The Art of Basket Making' (Putnam). Write: Robert Hamilton, Box 100, Manotick, Ontario, Canada

Panniers for Donkey in South Gloucestershire, new or good condition. Box No. 308 'The Countryman'

DIRECTORY OF USEFUL ADDRESSES

The Alpine Garden Society—for all those interested in rock gardens and alpine plants in the wild. Brochure from: 58 Denison House, 296 Vauxhall Bridge Road, S.W.1. 01-834 5037. Send 1/- Postage for free copy of Bulletin

Ancient Monuments Society, 12 Edwardes Square, London, W.8. Please apply for particulars

Berks. Bucks. and Oxfordshire Naturalists' Trust, Boswells, Wendover, Bucks. Works for the conservation of Wildlife in the three Counties

The British Bee-Keepers' Association. General Secretary: O. Meyer, 55 Chipstead Lane, Riverhead, Sevenoaks, Kent

British Waterfowl Association, Dept. C.M., Epping Upland, Essex, Tel.: Epping 5120 —for all interested in waterfowl. Subscription 25/- a year which includes quarterly Newsletter and expert advice

Cats' Protection League and Tailwavers, 29 Church Street, Slough (20173), Bucks.

Commons, Open Spaces and Footpaths Preservation Society, 166 Shaftesbury Avenue, W.C.2

The Council for Nature, Zoological Gardens, Regent's Park, London, N.W.1. Tel.: 722 7111, is the national representative body of the voluntary natural history movement in the United Kingdom. Information Service: monthly newsletter 'habitat', Subscription £1, Associates £5

Council for the Protection of Rural England: 4 Hobart Place, London, S.W.1

The Cremation Society (not conducted for profit), 47 Nottingham Place, W.1. (01-935 6079). Membership provides cremation facilities at any of the 204 crematoria. In 1969 339,000 cremations (53%) were carried out. Send for Booklet C2

Field Studies Council, 9 Devereux Court, Strand, London, WC2R. 3JR. Residential one week courses for Naturalists and Artists at nine Centres in England and Wales from March to November

The Folk-lore Society, c/o University College, Gower Street, London, W.C.1. (01-387 5894). Established 1878 to study and record traditional beliefs and practices of the people. Annual subscription, including quarterly journal 'Folklore', £3 3s 0d

Institute of Advanced Motorists Ltd. Empire House, Chiswick, London, W.4. Conducts the Advanced Driving Test. Tel.: 01-994 4403

Lake District Naturalists' Trust Limited, Bleak House, Windermere. Conserves wild life in the Lake District. Enquiries welcomed

The National Association of Flower Arrangement Societies of Great Britain, The Secretary, 21a Denbigh Street, London, S.W.1. 01-828 5145

The National Childbirth Trust. Modern approach to preparation for childbirth available to town and country dwellers alike. Write to Dept. C, 9 Queensborough Terrace, London, W.2

continued on page 413

RECOMMENDED NURSERYMEN

No entries are accepted for this section unless we are satisfied that the nurserymen listed provide good service, healthy plants and at reasonable prices. Your comments will help us.

DOBIE'S SEED BOOK

Be sure of getting Britain's Best Seed Book—130 pages offering the finest selection of garden seeds—all at money saving prices. Send today for your free copy to:
SAMUEL DOBIE & SON LTD., (Dept. Z761) 11 Grosvenor Street, Chester.

Alpines, Primulas, Ericas, Dwarf Shrubs. Many unusual plants stocked. Lists 1/-.
Edrom Nurseries, Coldingham, Eyemouth, Berwickshire

HEATHERS

Open Ground Plants in 100 Varieties to give Flowers throughout the year. Also Trees and Shrubs. Apply for Catalogues:—PLAS NEWYDD GARDENS, Llanfairpwll, Anglesey. Proprietor The MARQUESS OF ANGLESEY

Black & Flory Ltd., Orchids, Middle Green, Slough, Bucks. We specialise in orchids for the beginner as well as for the expert. Please write for current catalogue

Budding and Grafting Roses and Fruit Trees. Illustrated instructions with price list of stocks, scions, etc., sent on request. D. Stewart, Rose Grower, Arreton Nurseries, New Milton, Hampshire

---

PERRY'S OF ENFIELD

Perry's 1971 Catalogue of Shade-loving Plants and Hardy Ferns now ready, also Catalogue of Water Lilies, Aquatic Plants and Moisture-loving Plants. *Copies posted on application.*
PERRY'S HARDY PLANT FARM, ENFIELD, MIDDLESEX

Camellias to flower in succession from September to mid-Summer. Send 2/6d for 28 page descriptive list with cultural details. Treseders' Nurseries, Truro

Double Primroses, Old Laced Pinks, Alpines. Descriptive List 1/-. Mrs. McMurtrie, Balbithan House, Kintore, Aberdeenshire

---

LAURIES OF DUNDEE

The most extensive growers of top quality plants in Scotland. Flowering Trees and Shrubs, Roses, Heathers and Perennials. Catalogue 1/6d.
BLACKNESS NURSERY, NINEWELLS, DUNDEE

Heathers (Ericas, etc.). Wide variety, highest quality. Catalogue from Neil H. Brummage, Heathwoods Nursery, Taverham, Norwich

Orchids—Free Price-list. Charlesworth & Co. Ltd., Haywards Heath, Sussex

Strawberry Plants in Many Varieties and Types: Illustrated catalogue from Daymens Hill Nurseries, Tolleshunt Major, Maldon, Essex. Tiptree 327

HOSTAS. Our catalogue (price 1/-) has details of a large number of varieties. We also specialise in **RHODODENDRONS, AZALEAS** and **HEATHERS.**
HYDON NURSERIES LTD., HYDON HEATH, GODALMING, SURREY

Treneague Chamomile, Trevorder, Wadebridge, Cornwall. New flower-less Chamomile ground cover. Requires no cutting. Remains green, low spreading, fragrant. Easily propagated. 100 off-shoots 36/-

---

SHRUBS FROM SCOTLAND will enhance your enjoyment of your garden and increase its value. Choose from our large stocks of ornamental shrubs, rhododendrons, heaths and heathers and be delighted with the value you obtain for your money.
B. & D. ALEXANDER LTD., ARDENCAPLE NURSERIES, HELENSBURGH, SCOTLAND. Tel.: Helensburgh 4559. Colour Catalogue 1/-.

continued on page 412

RECOMMENDED NURSERYMEN—Continued

Note: It will be appreciated that some nurseries may not indicate in their advertisements the full range of the plants they offer. The Countryman is always willing to help readers with particular enquiries.

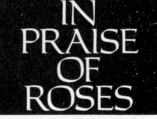

DIRECTORY OF USEFUL ADDRESSES—*continued from page 410*

The National Trust, 42 Queen Anne's Gate, London, S.W.1. Annual subscription £2

National Union of Agricultural and Allied Workers: Headland House, 308 Gray's Inn Road, London, W.C.1. Tel.: 01-278 7801

The Ramblers' Association, Dept. CM., 1/4 Crawford Mews, York Street, London, WIH IPT. Annual Subscription 10s 6d. Life Membership £10 10s 0d

The Royal Horticultural Society, Vincent Square. London, S.W.1. Anyone interested in horticulture may apply for Fellowship. Details from the Secretary

Scottish S.P.C.A. maintains 30 Inspectors (J. P. Constables) in 25 Scottish Counties. Send for 130th Annual Report. H.Q., 19 Melville Street, Edinburgh, EH3 7PL

The Society for the Protection of Ancient Buildings: 55 Great Ormond Street, WC1N 3JA

The Soil Association cares about farming, food and health and the future of man's environment, and provides a free advisory service to members. It publishes a quarterly journal and monthly newspaper (1/10d post free.) Further information from The Secretary, Walnut Tree Manor, Haughley, Stowmarket, Suffolk, IP14 3RS

Surrey Naturalists' Trust, Juniper Hall Field Centre, Dorking, works for conservation of wildlife. Membership £1 yearly. Volunteers welcome for active week-end work on our nature reserves. S.A.E. brings list of Christmas cards, notelets, calendars for country lovers

UFAW (The Universities Federation for Animal Welfare) 230 High Street, Potters Bar, Herts., provides a practical approach to the care of wild and domestic animals. Details on request

Wildlife Youth Service, Wallington, Surrey. (01-669 4995). Individual or Group Membership 5-18 years

The World Wildlife Fund. A charitable foundation devoted to conservation of wildlife and wild places for the benefit of man. It is dependent upon voluntary support. Information Service. Plumtree Court, London, E.C.4. Tel.: 01-353 2615

BOOKS FOR GARDENERS

By Margery Fish

A special money-saving offer!

Mrs. Margery Fish was a doyen of gardening writers, her books growing from her personal experience with her famous garden at East Lambrook Manor, near South Petherton, Somerset, which is to be preserved and kept open to the public.

By arrangement with the publishers we are offering five of her titles, all of them at a special price for our subscribers, apart from the newly-published **Gardening on Clay and Lime** (a book that could save much unnecessary hard work and bring joy to those whose gardens have sick soil), which has only just been published, for which we must therefore charge the regular price.

We made a garden How a novice created the now famous garden at East Lambrook. 120 pages, plus 8 plates. Published at 35/-, Countryman price 28/- post free.

Gardening in the shade Developing the peace and timelessness of a shady garden. 160 pages plus 16 plates. Published at 35/-, Countryman price 28/- post free.

Carefree Gardening How to achieve a trouble-free garden that is attractive all the year round. 150 pages plus 16 plates. Published at 35/-, Countryman price 28/- post free.

Ground Cover Plants Labour-saving plants and some interesting alternatives for grass. 144 pages plus 16 plates. Published at 35/-, Countryman price 28/- post free.

Gardening on Clay and Lime a newly-published work that will prove invaluable to those faced with clay or lime soils. 160 pages plus 16 plates. Price 35/- post free.

The Countryman, Book Offer MFC1, 23-27 Tudor St., London, EC4

The Development of Garden Flowers

RICHARD GORER

The first history of its kind, which traces the descent and development of well-known plants giving basic information on cultivation and plant breeding. Illus. 63s

EYRE & SPOTTISWOODE

THE COUNTRYMAN PHOTOGRAPHIC COMPETITION

Subject:

Life in a Village

RULES

1. Entries must illustrate an aspect of the theme 'Life in a Village'.
2. They must have been taken in Great Britain or Ireland on or after 1st January 1970 and must not have been published.
3. Prints must be black-and-white, unmounted, not less than $6\frac{1}{2}$ in. $\times$ $8\frac{1}{2}$ in. and not more than 10 in. $\times$ 12 in.
4. Up to three prints may be submitted with each signed entry form, which must include name and address, captions, dates and places of taking, camera and film. The number and caption must also be written in soft pencil on the back of each print. No paper-clips, please.
5. No *full-time* professional photographer and no member of the editorial staff of 'The Countryman' or relatives may enter the competition.
6. Entries must reach The Editor, 'The Countryman', Burford, Oxford, OX8 4LH, not later than 24th September 1971.
7. Prizewinners to be selected by Louis F. Peek, whose decision will be final. No entrant will be eligible for more than one prize. No correspondence will be entered into.
8. The results will be published in the Winter 1971 number of 'The Countryman'.
9. Entry of a photograph gives 'The Countryman' the exclusive right to reproduce it until 31st December 1972. The copyright will remain the property of the entrant. Prize-winning entries will be published without payment, but any others published will be paid for at the usual rates.
10. Prints, other than those retained for publication, will be returned to entrants if accompanied by a stamped and addressed envelope. All reasonable care will be taken, but neither 'The Countryman' nor the judge will be liable for loss of or damage to prints submitted.

ENTRY FORM IN SPRING AND SUMMER 1971